I0879116

# A Small Book for a Big Life

Living Large in a Small World

# A SMALL BOOK *for a* BIG LIFE

BRAD AHLQUIST

Ballast Books, LLC
www.ballastbooks.com

Copyright 2025 by Brad Ahlquist

All rights reserved. No part of this book may be reproduced in any form or by any electronic or mechanical means, including information storage and retrieval systems, without permission in writing from the publisher, except by reviewers, who may quote brief passages in a review.

ISBN 978-1-964934-41-9

Printed in Hong Kong

Published by Ballast Books
www.ballastbooks.com

For more information, bulk orders, appearances,
or speaking requests, please email: info@ballastbooks.com

# TABLE OF CONTENTS

# PREAMBLE

*A SMALL BOOK FOR A BIG LIFE* is a gentle reminder that it's the small, intentional choices we make every day that shape our lives and contribute to our overall happiness. It encourages readers to slow down, reflect on their values, and make conscious decisions that align with their true selves. With practical exercises, inspiring stories, and insightful guidance, this book serves as a roadmap for creating a life of meaning, connection, and personal fulfillment. Remember, a big life is not about grand gestures but about embracing the beauty and richness of each precious moment.

# PROLOGUE

WHEN I WAS in my early twenties, I had a small family of four (two boys and two girls), all under the age of ten, wanting to spend some family time together. I went out and bought a travel trailer to pull behind my Ford Bronco. Not being able to afford the mirror extensions required to pull such a trailer, I sought out my grandfather, who was a blacksmith and welder. I asked him if he would help me build a set of mirror extensions on my Bronco to pull my trailer. "Absolutely," he said. With that, I drove out to his shop, where we fashioned a set of mirror extensions.

During this process, as we were fitting the extensions and making the final adjustments, he asked me a simple question. In his strong Swedish accent, as he lifted his head and stared right at me, he said, "Bradley, where do you think you will be in five years' time?"

I quickly responded, "How the heck would I know?"

After finally getting the mirrors set right, I could easily see alongside the trailer with no blind spots. Best of all, I'd gotten this done for next to nothing. I felt very proud of what I had accomplished with his help, but as I was just getting ready to leave his shop, he asked me another series of questions.

"Where are you going camping?"

I told him.

"How far away is that?"

I told him.

"Can you make it on one tank of gas?"

No, I said, I would need to stop and fill up.

"Where?"

I told him.

"How long are you going to be gone?" he asked. "How many groceries will you need for the week?"

Through this conversation and back and forth, he became very confident that I had it all planned out to the minute and to the dollar. Again, I felt very proud of myself, as I had an immense respect for him and felt his approval resonating in his tone, right up until he commented, "Isn't it funny how we put more planning into our vacations than we do into our lives?"

And with that, he bid me a safe and fun-filled trip. As I drove away, and for the last forty-five years, this comment, the simple truth, has always been with me. He was 100 percent correct back then, and the comment is even more relevant today.

It wasn't that I did not *have* a plan for my future; the problem was I did not know *how* to plan for my future. Life was coming at me fast; it was all I could do to keep up. But if I had known how to plan, if I did know the simple truths of the wisdom of planning and setting goals, how much better could and would my life have been?

It is in this pursuit that I have written this small book. I hope it will help you, my dear reader, to maximize all that is good in your life and go on to live one that is happy and fulfilling.

So, let's get started planning the life you want to have, can have, and will have!

As Mark Twain so eloquently said, "The secret of getting ahead is getting started!"

ONE

# THE POWER OF GRATITUDE

*"Gratitude can transform common days into thanksgivings, turn routine jobs into joy, and change ordinary opportunities into blessings."*

—WILLIAM ARTHUR WARD

## Definition of Gratitude

GRATITUDE IS A heartfelt acknowledgment of the goodness in our lives. It involves recognizing and appreciating the blessings, experiences, and people that bring joy, meaning, and growth.

Once upon a time, in a quiet little village nestled between rolling hills and a meandering river, there lived an old man named Elias. He was known for his white beard, which flowed down to his chest, and his eyes that sparkled with the wisdom of countless years. Elias had seen many seasons come and go, and the weight of those years had left their mark on his back, which was slightly bent from the weight of time itself.

Elias lived a modest life in a small cottage by the riverbank. He was content with his daily routine, which consisted of tending to his small garden, reading books by the fire, and taking long walks along the river's edge. Despite his simple existence, Elias had a knack for seeing the beauty in life that often eluded others.

One cool autumn evening, as Elias sat by his fireplace, a visitor named Sarah arrived in the village. She had heard about the wise old man and his unique perspective on life, and she hoped to learn from him.

Elias welcomed her into his humble abode and offered her a warm cup of tea. They talked for hours, and Elias shared stories of his youth and the lessons he had learned over the years.

As the conversation flowed, Sarah noticed something remarkable about Elias. He had an air of contentment that seemed to radiate from his very being. She asked him, "Elias, what is the secret to your happiness and contentment in life? You seem so at peace with the world."

Elias smiled and said, "Ah, my dear, the secret is gratitude. I've come to realize that life is a precious gift, and there is beauty in every moment if you look for it. Gratitude is the key to unlocking that beauty."

Sarah was curious and asked, "But what is it about gratitude that makes life so beautiful?"

Elias leaned back in his chair, his eyes twinkling with wisdom. "Gratitude, my dear, allows you to see the good things even in the face of adversity. When you practice gratitude, you focus on the blessings rather than the burdens, on the joys rather than the sorrows. It changes your perspective and fills your heart with happiness."

Sarah pondered this for a moment and then asked, "But how can I learn to be more grateful like you, Elias?"

Elias chuckled softly and replied, "Gratitude is a practice, my dear. Start each day by counting your blessings, no matter how small they may seem. The warmth of the morning sun, the sound of birdsong, the smile of a passing stranger—all these are reasons to be thankful. And, in the evening, reflect on the day and find something to be grateful for. Over time, this practice will become a part of your being, and you'll begin to see the world through a more positive lens."

Sarah left Elias's cottage that day with a heart full of newfound wisdom. She made it a point to practice gratitude daily, just as Elias had advised. Slowly but surely, she noticed a change in herself. The world seemed to shine a little brighter, and her heart felt a little lighter.

Elias, with his white beard and age-old wisdom, continued to live his life by the riverbank, cherishing the simple pleasures that came his way. He knew that gratitude was the key to finding joy in life, and he shared this timeless wisdom with all who sought his guidance.

And so, in the quiet village nestled between rolling hills and a meandering river, Elias, the old man with a heart full of gratitude, continued to inspire others to find the beauty in the world and the goodness in their own hearts.

## UNDERSTANDING GRATITUDE

GRATITUDE IS A powerful and transformative mindset that involves recognizing and appreciating the positive aspects of life. It goes beyond simply saying "thank you" and delves into a deeper sense of acknowledgment and genuine appreciation. To truly understand gratitude, let's explore its essence and significance.

# GRATITUDE AS A TRANSFORMATIVE PRACTICE

GRATITUDE HAS THE power to transform our lives in profound ways. When practiced intentionally and consistently, gratitude can shift our mindset, enhance our well-being, and bring about positive changes in nearly every aspect of our lives. Let's explore how gratitude can be a transformative practice.

## Gratitude Shifts Focus to the Positive

WHEN WE PRACTICE gratitude, our attention is redirected from what is lacking or negative to the abundance and goodness in our lives. It helps us reframe our perspective and see the positive aspects even in challenging situations. By focusing on what we are grateful for, we cultivate a more optimistic outlook, learn to see the glass as half full rather than half empty, and attract more positivity into our lives.

## Gratitude Enhances Emotional Well-Being

MAKING GRATITUDE PART of our daily living boosts our emotional well-being by fostering beneficial emotions such as joy, contentment, and happiness. It helps counteract detrimental emotions like stress, anxiety, and dissatisfaction. Regular gratitude practice has been linked to increased levels of life satisfaction, improved mental health, and reduced symptoms of depression.

## Gratitude Cultivates Resilience

GRATITUDE STRENGTHENS OUR ability to bounce back from adversity and face challenges with resilience. When we appreciate the lessons and growth that come from difficult experiences, we develop a greater sense of inner strength and optimism for the future. Gratitude helps us reframe setbacks as opportunities for learning and personal development.

## Gratitude Deepens Relationships

EXPRESSING GRATITUDE TOWARD others deepens our relationships and fosters a sense of connection and appreciation. When we show appreciation for those around us, we acknowledge and value the contributions, support, and love we receive from others.

This strengthens bonds and creates a positive cycle of gratitude and kindness within our relationships.

### Gratitude Increases Empathy and Compassion

AS WE RECOGNIZE the kindness and generosity we receive, we become more attuned to the needs and struggles of others. Gratitude encourages acts of kindness and inspires us to make a positive difference in the lives of those around us.

### Gratitude Improves Physical Health

NOT ONLY DOES gratitude improve our emotional well-being but it has also been associated with improved physical health. Research suggests that practicing gratitude is linked to better sleep, reduced stress levels, a strengthened immune system, and lower blood pressure. The positive emotions generated through gratitude have a beneficial impact on our overall well-being.

### Gratitude Promotes Mindfulness and Presence

GRATITUDE PRACTICE ENCOURAGES us to be present in the moment and fully aware of the gifts and blessings in our lives. It helps us slow down, savor the present, and appreciate the simple joys and beauty that often go unnoticed. Gratitude enhances mindfulness and allows us to experience greater fulfillment in each moment.

### Gratitude Cultivates an Abundance Mentality

GRATITUDE SHIFTS OUR mindset from scarcity to abundance. It helps us recognize the richness and beauty that exist in our daily lives and allows us to see the abundance of resources, opportunities, and possibilities available to us. Instead of focusing on what we lack, we appreciate what we already have and open ourselves to receiving more blessings and opportunities.

### Gratitude Fosters Humility and Perspective

GRATITUDE OPENS US to the gift of humility and provides perspective. It reminds us of the interconnectedness of life and the contributions of others. It humbles us by acknowledging that we do not achieve success or happiness solely through our efforts but also through the support and opportunities provided by others.

### Gratitude Inspires Personal Growth

GRATITUDE FUELS PERSONAL growth by promoting self-reflection and introspection. When we express an appreciation for our strengths, achievements, and personal growth, we acknowledge our progress and feel inspired to continue evolving. Gratitude encourages us to embrace challenges, step out of our comfort zones, and pursue our goals with confidence.

## Gratitude Flows to Others

GRATITUDE IS CONTAGIOUS. When we embody an attitude of thankfulness and positivity, it has the power to influence those around us. Our appreciation and kindness inspire others to adopt a similar mindset, creating a ripple effect of gratitude in our families, communities, and beyond.

BY EMBRACING GRATITUDE as a transformative practice, we can experience profound shifts in our perspective, well-being, relationships, and overall quality of life. Through consistent gratitude practice, we open ourselves to a world of abundance, joy, and personal growth, and begin to see changes in the world around us.

# CULTIVATING AN ATTITUDE OF APPRECIATION

DEVELOPING AN ATTITUDE of appreciation involves actively recognizing and acknowledging the positive aspects of life. It's about shifting your perspective to focus on the abundance and blessings that surround you. The first step is to open your mind and create a space that will foster your growing gratitude mindset. Here are some strategies to help you cultivate an attitude of appreciation.

## Mindful Awareness

BEGIN BY BECOMING more mindful of your thoughts and emotions. Notice when negativity or complaints arise and consciously choose to redirect your attention to the positive aspects of your life. Practice being present in the moment and attuned to the beauty and goodness that exists around you.

## Shift Focus

INSTEAD OF DWELLING on what is lacking or not going well, intentionally focus on what you have and what is going right. Shift your attention to the abundance in your life, whether it's the relationships, opportunities, talents, or experiences that bring you joy and fulfillment.

## Practice Generosity

ENGAGE IN ACTS of kindness and generosity toward others. By giving to others, whether it's your time, support, or resources, you not only make a positive impact on their lives but also cultivate a sense of appreciation for your own ability to contribute and make a difference.

## Gratitude for Challenges

EMBRACE CHALLENGES AS opportunities for growth and learning. Instead of resenting or resisting them, approach them with a mindset of gratitude. Recognize that challenges provide valuable lessons, strength, and resilience, which can ultimately lead to personal development and achievement.

## Express Appreciation

TAKE THE TIME to express appreciation and gratitude to the people in your life. Show genuine gratitude for their presence, their support, and the positive impact they have on you. A simple "thank you" or a heartfelt expression of gratitude can go a long way in nurturing relationships and creating a positive atmosphere.

## Count Your Blessings

MAKE A HABIT of mentally counting your blessings regularly. Before you go to sleep or when you wake up in the morning, take a moment to reflect on the things you are grateful for. Remind yourself of the privileges, opportunities, and positive aspects of your life that you often take for granted.

## Nurture Optimism

DEVELOP A POSITIVE and optimistic outlook on life. Choose to see setbacks or disappointments as temporary and surmountable. Focus on the possibilities and potential for growth and improvement, even in challenging situations. This positive mindset cultivates an attitude of appreciation for the resilience and opportunities that arise.

## Surround Yourself with Positivity

SURROUND YOURSELF WITH people, experiences, and influences that uplift and inspire you. Seek out positive, like-minded individuals who appreciate and celebrate life's blessings. Engage in activities that bring you joy and fulfillment, and limit exposure to negative news or toxic environments that can dampen your appreciation.

## Practice Self-Reflection

TAKE TIME FOR self-reflection and introspection. Understand and appreciate your own strengths, accomplishments, and growth. Celebrate your progress and acknowledge the unique qualities that make you who you are.

## Gratitude Practice

ENGAGE IN REGULAR gratitude practices, such as keeping a gratitude journal or writing daily gratitude lists. Take time each day to reflect on and write down the things you appreciate and are grateful for. It can be as simple as a kind gesture from a friend, a delicious meal, or a beautiful sunset. This practice trains your mind to actively seek out the positive aspects of your life.

BY CONSISTENTLY PRACTICING these strategies, you can cultivate an attitude of appreciation that permeates your daily life. You'll find yourself more attuned to the positive aspects of life, experiencing greater joy, contentment, and a deeper sense of gratitude for the blessings that surround you.

# FINDING JOY IN EVERYDAY MOMENTS

LIFE IS FILLED with a multitude of small, ordinary moments that often go unnoticed. However, by practicing awareness and developing a sense of gratitude, we can uncover the joy and beauty hidden within these everyday experiences. Here are some ways to find joy in the simplicity of everyday life.

## Practice Mindfulness

ENGAGE IN THE practice of mindfulness, which involves being fully present in the current moment without judgment. By slowing down and paying attention to the details of your surroundings, you can discover moments of joy that may have previously passed unnoticed.

## Engage Your Senses

TAKE TIME TO appreciate the sensations that surround you. Notice the aroma of a freshly brewed cup of coffee, the warmth of sunlight on your skin, the sound of birds chirping, or the vibrant colors of flowers. Engaging your senses can heighten your awareness and bring joy to even the most mundane moments.

### Find Beauty in Nature

SPEND TIME OUTDOORS and connect with nature. Take a walk in a park, sit by a river, or simply gaze at the stars in the night sky. The beauty of nature has a way of inspiring awe and bringing a sense of joy and tranquility.

### Recognize Your Blessings

DEVELOP A MINDSET of gratitude for the small blessings in your life. Take a moment each day to reflect on the things you are grateful for, whether it's a supportive friend, a delicious meal, a cozy home, or a peaceful moment of solitude. Recognizing and appreciating these simple joys can bring immense happiness.

### Embrace Simple Pleasures

FIND JOY IN the simple activities that bring you happiness, such as reading a book, listening to music, cooking a meal, or spending quality time with loved ones. Appreciate the contentment and fulfillment that these activities can bring to your life.

### Practice Random Acts of Kindness

PERFORM ACTS OF kindness and generosity toward others. The joy that comes from making someone else's day brighter or easier is an incredible source of happiness. Whether it's offering a helping hand, sharing a compliment, or giving a small gift, acts of kindness can bring immense joy both to the receiver and the giver.

### Celebrate Milestones and Achievements

TAKE TIME TO acknowledge and celebrate your accomplishments, no matter how small they may seem. Whether it's completing a task, reaching a personal goal, or learning a new skill, recognizing your achievements can bring a sense of joy and fulfillment.

### Cultivate a Positive Mindset

TRAIN YOUR MIND to focus on the positive aspects of life. Practice reframing negative thoughts into more positive and empowering ones. By consciously choosing to see the bright side of situations, you can cultivate a mindset that is more open to joy and happiness.

### Seek Playfulness and Laughter

ALLOW YOURSELF TO let go and embrace moments of playfulness and laughter. Engage in activities that bring out your inner child, whether it's playing games, telling jokes, or spending time with playful pets. Laughter has a way of infusing joy into every aspect of life.

### Let Your Actions Express Gratitude

EXPRESS YOUR GRATITUDE to others through acts of appreciation and kindness. Thank someone for their help, send a heartfelt note of gratitude, or offer a sincere compliment. Showing gratitude not only uplifts others but also enhances your own sense of joy and connection.

FINDING JOY IN everyday moments requires a shift in perspective and a willingness to embrace the present moment. By incorporating these practices into your daily life, you can uncover the beauty, wonder, and joy that exists within the seemingly ordinary moments, leading to a more joyful and fulfilling life.

## GRATITUDE EXERCISES AND RITUALS

PRACTICING GRATITUDE EXERCISES and rituals can deepen our sense of appreciation and enhance our overall well-being. By intentionally cultivating gratitude, we can train our minds to focus on the positive aspects of life and develop a greater sense of contentment. Here are some exercises and rituals you can incorporate into your daily routine.

### Gratitude Journal

SET ASIDE A few minutes each day to write down three to five things you are grateful for. Reflect on the specific people, experiences, or blessings that brought you joy or made a positive impact on your life. Write in detail expressing why you are grateful for each item. Regularly revisiting your gratitude journal can serve as a reminder of the abundance in your life.

## Gratitude Letter

CHOOSE SOMEONE YOU deeply appreciate and write them a heartfelt gratitude letter. Express your sincere thanks, letting them know how they have positively influenced your life. You can either send the letter or read it to them in person. This exercise not only fosters gratitude but also strengthens relationships and spreads positivity.

## Three Good Things

BEFORE GOING TO bed, reflect on three good things that happened during the day. They can be simple moments or significant events. Write them down or simply mentally acknowledge them. This exercise shifts your focus toward positive experiences and can improve your overall well-being.

## Gratitude Walk

TAKE A MINDFUL walk in nature, focusing on the beauty and wonders around you. As you stroll, consciously express gratitude for the elements you encounter. Appreciate the colors, scents, sounds, and textures. This practice deepens your connection to the natural world and cultivates a sense of gratitude for its abundant gifts.

## Gratitude Meditation

FIND A QUIET space and dedicate a few minutes to a gratitude meditation. Close your eyes, take deep breaths, and focus your attention on the things you are grateful for. With each breath, allow the feelings of gratitude to expand within you. Visualize the people, experiences, and blessings that fill you with appreciation and let that gratitude infuse your entire being.

## Gratitude Jar

PLACE A JAR and small slips of paper in a visible location in your home. Each day, write down a moment of gratitude or something you are thankful for on a slip of paper and place it in the jar. Over time, the jar will fill with reminders of the abundance in your life. When you need a boost of positivity, revisit the jar and read through the slips of gratitude.

## Gratitude Sharing at Meals

BEFORE EACH MEAL, take a moment to share something you are grateful for with your family or friends. It can be as simple as expressing gratitude for the food, the company, or the opportunity to gather. This practice establishes a mindful and grateful atmosphere during mealtime.

### Gratitude Alarms or Reminders

SET ALARMS OR reminders on your phone or computer throughout the day. When the reminder pops up, pause for a moment and reflect on something you are grateful for in that moment. These gentle prompts serve as regular cues to cultivate gratitude amidst the busyness of daily life.

### Gratitude Rituals

CREATE PERSONAL GRATITUDE rituals that resonate with you. It could be lighting a candle and taking a moment to express thanks, creating a gratitude jar filled with symbolic items that represent moments of appreciation, or saying a short gratitude prayer or affirmation each morning. These rituals help anchor gratitude in your daily life.

### Gratitude Circle

GATHER A GROUP of friends or family members for a gratitude circle. Sit in a circle and take turns sharing something you are grateful for. This ritual creates a supportive and uplifting environment while fostering a deeper sense of gratitude and connection.

REMEMBER, CONSISTENCY IS key when practicing gratitude exercises and rituals. Gratitude is a practice that can be cultivated intentionally. It involves consciously seeking and acknowledging moments of gratitude, whether through keeping a gratitude journal, sharing gratitude with loved ones, or simply reflecting on what we are grateful for each day.

Understanding gratitude is the first step toward embracing its transformative power in our lives. By incorporating gratitude into our daily routines and interactions, we can experience greater joy, contentment, and a deeper appreciation for the blessings that surround us.

# TWO

# CULTIVATING MINDFULNESS

*"Be where you are, not where you think you should be."*

—UNKNOWN

IN A QUAINT, sun-dappled village, there lived an old man named Samuel. He was known for his serene demeanor and a presence that seemed to emanate a profound sense of peace. Every morning without fail, Samuel could be found sitting by the village's tranquil pond, his eyes closed and a faint smile on his face. The villagers often wondered about his unusual morning ritual.

One day, a curious young boy named Lucas gathered the courage to approach Samuel and ask him about his daily routine.

"What are you doing by the pond every morning, sir?" Lucas inquired.

Samuel opened his eyes, and his kind gaze met Lucas's curious one.

"I'm practicing being in the present, my young friend," he replied with a gentle smile. "It's a way of fully immersing oneself in the moment, free from distractions and preoccupations."

Lucas was intrigued and asked, "Why is it important to be in the present?"

Samuel motioned for Lucas to sit beside him. "You see, young one, life can pass us by in a blur if we're not careful. The world is full of distractions, the worries of the past and the anxieties about the future.

We forget to fully experience the beauty and wonders that exist right in front of us. Being in the present allows us to appreciate the here and now, to find joy in the simple things, and to truly live each moment."

Lucas listened intently, and with Samuel's guidance, he decided to give it a try. The next morning, he joined the old man by the pond, closed his eyes, and took a deep breath. The gentle rustle of the leaves, the chirping of the birds, and the ripple of the water became his focus. He felt a sense of calm wash over him, and for the first time, he noticed the world with newfound clarity.

Days turned into weeks, and Lucas continued his practice of being in the present. He soon realized that mindfulness wasn't just about sitting by the pond; it was about carrying that sense of presence into every aspect of his life. When he ate, he savored each bite and the flavors that danced on his tongue. When he walked, he felt the earth beneath his feet and the warmth of the sun on his skin.

Lucas discovered that by being fully present, he could connect more deeply with the people around him. He listened to his family's stories without his mind wandering, and he shared their laughter with his whole heart. When he played with his friends, he immersed himself in the joy of the moment, free from concerns about the past or future.

As time went by, Lucas noticed a transformation within himself. The worries that had once plagued his thoughts became less burdensome, and he found peace in the simplicity of life. He realized that being in the present was not an escape from reality but a way of embracing it fully.

Lucas shared his newfound wisdom with the villagers, and many joined him and Samuel by the pond, practicing mindfulness together. The village began to bloom with a sense of harmony and connectedness that had been absent for years.

Samuel watched with pride as the village transformed, a testament to the power of being in the present. He knew that in the hustle and bustle of life, the practice of mindfulness was a precious gift that allowed people to savor each moment and truly live.

## THE ART OF BEING PRESENT

BEING PRESENT IS the practice of fully immersing yourself in the present moment, free from distractions and preoccupations. It involves cultivating mindfulness and a deep awareness of the here and now. Here are some strategies to help you master the art of being present.

### Cultivate Mindfulness

MINDFULNESS IS THE foundation of being present. Practice bringing your attention to the present moment without judgment. Focus on your senses, your breath, or the task at hand. Engage in mindfulness meditation or other mindfulness exercises to enhance your ability to stay present.

### Let Go of the Past and Future

RELEASE ATTACHMENTS TO the past and worries about the future. Recognize that the only moment you truly have control over is the present. Accept the past as something that has already happened and the future as uncertain. Shift your focus to the present moment and embrace its possibilities.

### Engage in Single-Tasking

INSTEAD OF MULTITASKING, strive for single-tasking. Dedicate your attention and energy to one task at a time, fully immersing yourself in the experience. Whether it's working, eating, or spending time with loved ones, be fully present and give your undivided attention to the task or person in front of you.

### Participate in Active Listening

WHEN ENGAGED IN conversations, practice active listening. Give your full attention to the speaker, maintain eye contact, and truly hear their words. Avoid planning your response or getting lost in your thoughts. Stay present and genuinely connect with the person speaking.

### Observe and Appreciate the Present Moment

TAKE THE TIME to observe and appreciate the details of your surroundings. Notice the sights, sounds, smells, and textures. Engage your senses fully and immerse yourself in the present moment. Find beauty and joy in the simple things that often go unnoticed.

## Embrace Mindful Movement

ENGAGE IN MINDFUL movement practices such as yoga, tai chi, or walking meditation. These activities help bring your focus to the sensations of your body and the present moment. Pay attention to each movement, your breath, and the sensations you experience.

## Create Mindful Transitions

INCORPORATE MINDFUL TRANSITIONS into your daily routines. Before moving from one activity to another, take a moment to pause, breathe, and consciously shift your attention. Use these moments as an opportunity to reset and ground yourself in the present before moving forward.

## Set Boundaries with Technology

LIMIT YOUR EXPOSURE to technology and digital distractions. Create boundaries by setting designated times for checking emails, social media, or other online activities. When engaging with technology, do so mindfully and with intention rather than mindlessly consuming information.

## Be Kind to Yourself

BE GENTLE AND compassionate with yourself as you cultivate the art of being present. It is a practice that requires patience and consistent effort. Release judgment and allow yourself to fully experience each moment, embracing both the joys and challenges that arise.

## Opportunities for Practicing Gratitude

IN YOUR QUEST to cultivate mindfulness, it will help to have gratitude for the present moment and the experiences it brings. Take the time to reflect on what you appreciate and are grateful for in your life. Gratitude helps you shift your focus to the positive aspects of the present moment and enhances your overall sense of well-being.

REMEMBER, BEING PRESENT is not about eliminating thoughts or emotions but rather acknowledging them without becoming entangled in them. By practicing the art of being present, you can enhance your overall well-being, deepen your connections, and find greater peace and fulfillment in the richness of each moment.

# PRACTICES FOR CULTIVATING MINDFULNESS

MINDFULNESS IS A state of active and nonjudgmental awareness of the present moment. Cultivating mindfulness can help you reduce stress, enhance focus, and develop a deeper sense of well-being. Here are some practices to help you cultivate mindfulness in your daily life.

## Mindful Breathing

PAY ATTENTION TO your breath as it flows in and out. Focus your awareness on the sensations of each breath—the coolness of the inhale and the warmth of the exhale. Whenever your mind wanders, gently bring your attention back to the breath.

## Body Scan Meditation

TAKE A FEW moments to scan your body from head to toe, noticing any sensations or areas of tension. Bring a sense of gentle curiosity to each part of your body without judgment. This practice helps you connect with your physical sensations and cultivate awareness of your body.

### Mindful Eating

SLOW DOWN AND savor each bite of your meals. Engage all your senses, paying attention to the smell, taste, texture, and colors of the food. Pay attention to the sensations of chewing and swallowing. Notice any thoughts or emotions that arise as you eat.

### Walking Meditation

TAKE A WALK with the intention of being fully present. Focus on the sensation of each step—the feeling of your feet touching the ground, the movement of your body, and the sights and sounds around you. Allow yourself to be immersed in the experience of walking.

### Mindful Observation

CHOOSE AN OBJECT, such as a flower, a piece of artwork, or a natural scene. Observe it with focused attention, noticing its details, colors, and shapes. Engage your senses fully and allow yourself to be absorbed in the present moment.

## Mindful Journaling

SET ASIDE TIME to reflect on your experiences and thoughts through journaling. Write without judgment, allowing your thoughts and emotions to flow onto the pages. Notice any patterns or insights that arise as you engage in this mindful practice.

## Loving-Kindness Meditation

CULTIVATE FEELINGS OF love, compassion, and kindness towards yourself and others. Begin by directing these feelings towards yourself, then gradually expand them to include loved ones, acquaintances, and even challenging individuals. Repeat phrases of goodwill and compassion as you hold each person in your awareness.

## Mindful Media Consumption

BE INTENTIONAL ABOUT your media consumption. Before engaging with television, social media, or other forms of media, check in with yourself and set an intention for how you want to engage with them mindfully. Notice your reactions and emotions as you consume media and consider how it affects your well-being.

## Mindful Pause

THROUGHOUT YOUR DAY, take mindful pauses to bring yourself into the present moment. Pause and take a few deep breaths, allowing yourself to rest and recenter. Use these pauses as reminders to bring awareness to your thoughts, feelings, and surroundings.

## Mindful Relationships

PRACTICE MINDFUL LISTENING and presence in your interactions with others. Give your full attention to the person you're speaking with, truly hearing and understanding their words. Be present with them without the need to judge or respond immediately. Cultivate empathy and understanding in your relationships.

REMEMBER, MINDFULNESS IS a skill that develops with practice. Start by incorporating these practices into your daily routine in small doses and gradually expand them as you feel comfortable. By cultivating mindfulness, you can bring a greater sense of presence, awareness, and peace into your life.

# FINDING PEACE IN THE MIDST OF CHAOS

LIFE OFTEN PRESENTS us with challenges and chaotic situations that can disrupt our sense of inner peace. However, it is possible to cultivate a sense of peace even in the midst of chaos. Here are some practices that can help you find peace during turbulent times.

## Practice Mindfulness

CULTIVATE PRESENT-MOMENT AWARENESS through mindfulness. Bring your attention to the here and now, accepting the present moment as it is without judgment. By grounding yourself in the present, you can find peace regardless of external circumstances.

## Deep Breathing and Relaxation

WHEN FACED WITH chaos, take intentional deep breaths to calm your nervous system. Engage in relaxation techniques such as progressive muscle relaxation, guided imagery, or deep breathing exercises to release tension and promote a state of inner calm.

### Acceptance and Letting Go

PRACTICE ACCEPTANCE OF the situation as it is, acknowledging that some things are beyond your control. Let go of the need to control or change external circumstances and focus instead on accepting and responding to the present moment with grace and equanimity.

### Self-Care and Boundaries

PRIORITIZE SELF-CARE TO nurture your well-being amidst chaos. Set healthy boundaries by identifying and respecting your limits. Take breaks, engage in activities that bring you joy, and make time for self-reflection and self-care practices that replenish your energy.

### Find Solace in Nature

CONNECT WITH THE healing power of nature. Spend time outdoors, whether it's a walk in a park, sitting near a body of water, or simply appreciating the beauty of the natural world. Nature has a calming effect on the mind and can provide a sense of peace and perspective.

### Seek Support

REACH OUT TO loved ones or a support network during challenging times. Sharing your feelings and experiences with trusted individuals can provide emotional support and a sense of comfort. Consider seeking professional help or counseling if needed.

### Engage in Mindful Activities

ENGAGE IN ACTIVITIES that promote mindfulness and bring you joy. This could include hobbies, creative pursuits, physical exercise, or engaging in activities that allow you to fully immerse yourself in the present moment. Find what brings you peace and make time for it regularly.

### Embrace Impermanence

REMEMBER THAT CHAOS and difficult times are temporary. Embrace the understanding that change is a constant in life. Remind yourself that this too shall pass and that you have the resilience to navigate through challenging situations.

## Inner Reflection and Self-Compassion

TAKE TIME FOR inner reflection and self-compassion. Offer yourself kindness, understanding, and compassion during chaotic times. Practice self-compassion by treating yourself with the same care and understanding you would offer to a close friend.

## Opportunities for Practicing Gratitude

CULTIVATE A GRATITUDE practice to shift your focus toward the positive aspects of your life. Regularly acknowledge and appreciate the things you are grateful for, even amidst chaos. Gratitude helps cultivate a positive mindset and promotes inner peace.

FINDING PEACE IN the midst of chaos is a personal journey that requires patience and self-awareness. Embrace these practices and adapt them to your unique circumstances. By nurturing your inner peace, you can navigate through chaos with greater resilience, calmness, and clarity.

## THREE

# EMBRACING AUTHENTICITY

*"Only the truth of who you are,*
*if realized, will set you free."*

—ECKHART TOLLE

IN A BUSTLING city, amidst the towering skyscrapers and the never-ending rush of people, there lived a woman named Susan. From a young age, she had a unique gift that set her apart from the crowd: a mesmerizing voice that could move hearts and stir souls. But Susan's gift remained hidden, locked behind the bars of self-doubt and societal expectations.

Susan came from a family of doctors, and it was expected that she would follow in their footsteps. Despite her natural talent for singing, she was led to believe that pursuing a career in music was impractical and risky. The cacophony of societal expectations and her own self-limiting beliefs had confined her to a career in medicine, far from the stage she secretly longed for.

Years passed, and Susan found herself working long hours at a prestigious hospital. While she was a skilled nurse, the gnawing feeling of unfulfillment never left her. Her gift and her passion for singing were like a caged bird longing to soar free.

One evening, Susan had a chance encounter with an old friend from her school choir. As they reminisced about their shared love for music, Susan felt a spark of inspiration. She realized that she had been living her life according to others' expectations and her own self-imposed limitations. It was time to break free.

With unwavering determination, Susan decided to pursue her true self by embracing her unique gift coupled with her passion for singing. She began performing at local open mic nights. Her voice, filled with emotion and authenticity, captured the hearts of those who listened.

As she broke free from societal expectations and her own fears, Susan's talent began to shine brighter. She knew that to achieve greatness, she needed to live in alignment with her values and embrace her true self.

Susan's journey was not without its hardships. She faced moments of self-doubt. But her gift, her voice, had an uncanny ability to connect with people on a profound level.

One day, Susan decided to take action at a local talent hunt contest. She mustered her nerves and, putting her age aside, decided to enter and give it her all. She took charge of her actions and sang her heart out on that big stage. At first, she stood silent, waiting for her cue. Then she opened her mouth and sang, "I dreamed a dream in time gone by . . ." The audience was shocked—her voice was that of a thousand angels. She finished the song to a standing ovation. She had completed her task and was proud of overcoming all her fears in one fell swoop. With that, she proudly began to walk off the stage. The judges, shocked, called out to her to return.

As Susan stood on the grand stage, she knew that she had achieved greatness not just through her music but also through her unwavering commitment to being true to herself. The world had witnessed the extraordinary power of unleashing one's true self and embracing one's unique gifts and passions.

Susan's story became an inspiration to many who had suppressed their own gifts and passions, fearing the judgment of others and their own limitations. She showed them that by breaking free from societal expectations and self-limiting beliefs, by embracing their true selves and living in alignment with their values and purpose, they could achieve greatness beyond their wildest dreams.

Susan has gone on to establish herself as a true international star. People come from all over the world to attend her concerts. She is living her passion and purpose at last.

## UNLEASHING YOUR TRUE SELF

UNLEASHING YOUR TRUE self is about embracing your authentic nature, expressing your unique gifts and passions, and living in alignment with your values and purpose. It involves breaking free from societal expectations, self-limiting beliefs, and fears that hold you back. Here are some key principles to help you unleash your true self.

### Exercise Self-Reflection and Self-Awareness

TAKE TIME FOR self-reflection to gain a deeper understanding of who you are at your core. Explore your values, strengths, passions, and aspirations. Cultivate self-awareness by noticing your thoughts, emotions, and behaviors. This self-discovery process lays the foundation for embracing your true self.

### Embrace Authenticity

EMBRACE YOUR AUTHENTIC self by honoring your true thoughts, feelings, and desires. Let go of the need to please others or conform to societal expectations. Embrace your quirks, uniqueness, and imperfections. Authenticity empowers you to live a life that is genuine and aligned with your true essence.

### Identify Your Passions and Purpose

DISCOVER YOUR PASSIONS and purpose in life. Explore activities, interests, and causes that ignite a fire within you. When you align your life with your passions and purpose, you tap into a source of inspiration, fulfillment, and personal power.

### Overcome Fear and Limiting Beliefs

IDENTIFY AND CHALLENGE the fears and limiting beliefs that hold you back from expressing your true self. Replace self-doubt with self-belief and embrace a growth mindset. Take small steps outside your comfort zone, gradually expanding your boundaries and realizing that you are capable of more than you may think.

### Nurture Self-Compassion

PRACTICE SELF-COMPASSION BY treating yourself with kindness, understanding, and forgiveness. Embrace your strengths and accept your flaws. Celebrate your achievements and learn from your mistakes. Self-compassion nurtures self-acceptance and allows you to authentically express yourself without harsh self-judgment.

### Surround Yourself with Supportive People

SURROUND YOURSELF WITH people who accept and support you for who you truly are. Seek out relationships that encourage your growth, authenticity, and self-expression. Connect with individuals who inspire and uplift you and let go of toxic relationships that stifle your true self.

### Take Inspired Action

ONCE YOU HAVE gained clarity about your true self, passions, and purpose, take inspired action to manifest your authentic desires. Set goals that align with your true self and take steps toward achieving them. Embrace the courage to follow your dreams and make choices that reflect your authentic voice.

### Embrace Growth and Learning

EMBRACE A MINDSET of continuous growth and learning. Stay open to new experiences, perspectives, and opportunities for self-improvement. Embracing growth allows you to evolve and adapt while staying true to your core values and authentic self.

### Opportunities for Practicing Gratitude and Mindfulness

PRACTICE GRATITUDE FOR your journey and the opportunities that allow you to unleash your true self. Express appreciation for your strengths, passions, and the people who support you. Gratitude keeps you grounded, humble, and connected to the abundance of life.

Practicing mindfulness will help you stay connected to the present moment and to your authentic self. Mindfulness helps you observe and accept your thoughts and emotions without judgment. It allows you to make conscious choices aligned with your true values and aspirations.

UNLEASHING YOUR TRUE self is a lifelong journey of self-discovery, growth, and self-expression. It requires courage, vulnerability, and a commitment to living authentically. Embrace your uniqueness, follow your heart, and let your true self shine brightly in the world.

# OVERCOMING THE FEAR OF JUDGMENT

THE FEAR OF judgment is a common obstacle that can hinder personal growth, self-expression, and the pursuit of our goals and dreams. Here are some strategies and practices to help overcome the fear of judgment.

## Recognize the Fear

ACKNOWLEDGE AND UNDERSTAND that the fear of judgment is a normal human experience. Realize that many people experience similar fears and that it does not define your worth or abilities.

## Challenge Your Assumptions

EXAMINE THE BELIEFS and assumptions that underlie your fear of judgment. Are they based on actual evidence or more on your perception? Question whether the opinions of others truly hold the power to determine your self-worth and happiness.

## Embrace Imperfection

ACCEPT THAT PERFECTION is an unrealistic expectation. Understand that making mistakes and facing criticism are parts of the learning and growing process. Embrace imperfections as opportunities for improvement and see them as stepping stones to success.

## Focus on Self-Validation

SHIFT YOUR FOCUS from seeking validation from others to validating yourself. Develop a strong sense of self-worth and self-acceptance. Remind yourself of your strengths, accomplishments, and the value you bring to the world.

## Build a Community of Support

SEEK OUT SUPPORTIVE and encouraging individuals who uplift and inspire you. Surround yourself with people who appreciate and accept you for who you are. Their positive influence can help counteract your fear of judgment.

## Face Your Fears with Self-Compassion

TREAT YOURSELF WITH kindness and understanding. Be compassionate toward your own thoughts and feelings. Offer yourself the same level of empathy and support you would provide to a friend facing similar fears.

### Reframe Failure

SHIFT YOUR PERSPECTIVE on failure. Instead of viewing it as a reflection of your worth, see it as an opportunity for growth and learning. Embrace a growth mindset where setbacks are seen as stepping stones toward improvement and eventual success.

### Keep Your Mind on Your Goals and Passions

DIRECT YOUR ATTENTION and energy toward your goals, passions, and values. When you are deeply committed to something meaningful, the fear of judgment becomes less significant. Focus on your own progress and fulfillment rather than seeking external validation.

### Engage in Self-Expression

SEEK OUT AND participate in activities that allow you to express yourself authentically. Write, create art, speak in public, or engage in hobbies that allow you to showcase your unique talents and perspectives. Gradually expose yourself to situations that challenge your fear of judgment.

## Challenge Negative Self-Talk

BECOME AWARE OF negative self-talk and the inner critic that fuels the fear of judgment. Replace self-defeating thoughts with positive and affirming statements. Remind yourself of your worth and capabilities.

## Seek Feedback from Trusted Sources

INSTEAD OF FEARING judgment from everyone, seek constructive feedback from trusted individuals whose opinions you value and respect. Focus on feedback that can help you grow and improve.

## Take Small Steps

GRADUALLY EXPOSE YOURSELF to situations that trigger the fear of judgment. Start with small steps and progressively increase the challenge. Each successful experience will boost your confidence and diminish the fear.

## Opportunities for Practicing Gratitude and Mindfulness

AS YOU FACE your fear of judgment head-on, you'll have many opportunities to practice gratitude. Be grateful for both your successes and perceived failures, as each one is a step in the right direction.

Practicing mindfulness will help you observe your fear of judgment without judgment itself. Notice the thoughts and emotions that arise when you feel judged, and then let them pass without attaching too much significance to them. Stay grounded in the present moment.

REMEMBER THAT OVERCOMING the fear of judgment is a process that takes time and practice. Be patient with yourself and celebrate your progress along the way. Embrace your uniqueness, trust in your abilities, and focus on living a fulfilling life aligned with your values and aspirations.

# EMBRACING VULNERABILITY AND SELF-ACCEPTANCE

EMBRACING VULNERABILITY AND self-acceptance is essential for living a wholehearted and authentic life. It allows you to connect with your true self, foster deeper relationships, and experience a greater sense of fulfillment. Here are some strategies to help you embrace vulnerability and self-acceptance.

## Recognize the Power of Vulnerability

UNDERSTAND THAT VULNERABILITY is not a weakness but a courageous act of authenticity. It involves showing up as your true self even when it feels uncomfortable or uncertain. Recognize that vulnerability is a gateway to meaningful connections, personal growth, and a richer, more fulfilling life.

## Approach Growth with Self-Compassion

CULTIVATE SELF-COMPASSION BY treating yourself with kindness, understanding, and acceptance.

Be gentle with yourself when facing challenges or making mistakes. Embrace your imperfections and recognize that they are part of what makes you unique and human. Offer yourself the same compassion and understanding you would extend to a loved one.

### Challenge Perfectionism

LET GO OF the need for perfection and the unrealistic expectations you may place on yourself. Embrace the idea that making mistakes and experiencing setbacks is a natural part of growth and learning. Allow yourself to be vulnerable by acknowledging your limitations and embracing the process of continuous improvement.

### Celebrate Your Strengths

FOCUS ON YOUR strengths, talents, and accomplishments. Acknowledge and celebrate the unique qualities and abilities that make you who you are. Embracing your strengths boosts your self-confidence and provides a foundation for embracing vulnerability and self-acceptance.

### Seek Supportive Relationships

SURROUND YOURSELF WITH individuals who create a safe and nonjudgmental space for you to be yourself.

Seek out supportive friends, family members, or a therapist who can offer empathy, understanding, and encouragement. Having a support network that values and accepts you can greatly enhance your ability to embrace vulnerability and self-acceptance.

### Express Your Authentic Self

ALLOW YOURSELF TO express your thoughts, feelings, and desires openly and honestly. Communicate your needs, boundaries, and aspirations without fear of judgment or rejection. When you authentically express yourself, you create opportunities for deeper connections and attract people who appreciate and accept you for who you truly are.

### Embrace Mistakes and Learn from Failure

SHIFT YOUR PERSPECTIVE on mistakes and failures. View them as valuable learning experiences rather than personal shortcomings. Embrace the vulnerability of trying new things, even if failure is a possibility. Recognize that growth and resilience come from learning, adapting, and moving forward after setbacks.

## Set Healthy Boundaries

ESTABLISH CLEAR BOUNDARIES that protect your emotional well-being and allow you to honor your authentic self. Learn to say no to things that don't align with your values or drain your energy. Setting boundaries empowers you to prioritize self-care, respect your needs, and create space for vulnerability and self-acceptance.

## Opportunities for Practicing Gratitude and Mindfulness

REMEMBER TO PRACTICE gratitude for yourself and the journey of self-acceptance. Recognize the progress you have made, the strengths you possess, and the experiences that have shaped you. Practice gratitude for the lessons learned through vulnerability and self-discovery. Gratitude helps foster a positive and accepting mindset.

Practice mindfulness to become aware of your thoughts, emotions, and vulnerabilities without judgment. Observe your inner dialogue and gently challenge any self-critical or negative beliefs that arise. Mindfulness helps you develop a nonjudgmental and accepting attitude toward yourself and others.

REMEMBER, EMBRACING VULNERABILITY and self-acceptance is a lifelong journey. It requires ongoing practice, patience, and self-reflection. By embracing vulnerability, accepting yourself as you are, and showing up authentically, you open yourself to deeper connections and personal growth.

FOUR

# PURSUING PASSIONS AND PURPOSE

*"There is no passion to be found playing small—
in settling for a life that is less than the one you are
capable of living."*

—NELSON MANDELA

IN A QUAINT town nestled by the sea, there lived a man named James. For as long as he could remember, James had been living a life guided by the expectations of others. He had a secure job at a local bank, a respectable but uninspiring career. However, he carried within him an unfulfilled longing, a curiosity that he had suppressed for years.

James's journey of self-exploration and self-discovery began on a seemingly ordinary day. He happened upon an old bookshop with a weathered sign that read "Curiosities and Wonders." The moment he stepped inside, he was transported to a world of forgotten treasures and hidden knowledge. The musty smell of old books and the soft creaking of wooden floors spoke to his soul.

As he wandered through the narrow aisles, a particular book caught his attention. It was a thick volume about ancient maps and explorers filled with tales of uncharted territories and forgotten realms. James had always been fascinated by maps, and he realized that his passion for exploration was still very much alive, buried beneath the surface.

With the book in hand, he began studying maps in his free time. He marveled at the artistry of cartography and the stories held within each line and symbol. His fascination led him to learn about geology, history, and cultures from around the world. The more he delved into this newfound passion, the more he realized that his heart had found its true calling.

Driven by his desire to explore and map the uncharted territories of his own life, James made a life-altering decision. He decided to leave his secure job at the bank and set out on a journey of self-discovery and adventure. His friends and family were astonished by his sudden decision, unable to fathom why he would leave behind a stable career for the uncertain path of exploration.

James's journey took him to remote corners of the world, from the Amazon rainforest to the frozen tundra of the Arctic. He trekked through dense jungles, scaled towering mountains, and ventured into unknown caves. His unique desires, curiosities, and talents were in full bloom as he immersed himself in the thrill of exploration.

With each expedition, he felt a profound sense of fulfillment. He was capturing the beauty of unexplored landscapes through his maps and photographs, and in the process, he was discovering his own authentic self. The joy of exploration, the connection to nature, and the fulfillment of pursuing his true passion filled his days with purpose.

But the path was not without its challenges. He faced moments of solitude, uncertainty, and physical hardships. There were times when he longed for the comfort and security of his old life. However, James knew that the journey of self-discovery was the only way to live authentically, and he pressed on.

As the years passed, James became a renowned explorer and cartographer. His work was celebrated not only for its accuracy but also for its artistry. The maps he created were considered works of art, and his expeditions were seen as a testament to the power of self-discovery and pursuing one's true passions.

James's story became an inspiration for those who longed to explore their own interests and discover their true selves. He proved that the journey of self-exploration could lead to a life filled with purpose, happiness, and a profound sense of authenticity. By tapping into his unique desires, curiosities, and talents, James had not only discovered the world but also himself, and in doing so, he had found complete fulfillment.

# DISCOVERING YOUR PASSIONS AND INTERESTS

DISCOVERING YOUR PASSIONS and interests is a journey of self-exploration and self-discovery. It involves tapping into your unique desires, curiosities, and talents. Here are some strategies to help you uncover and embrace your passions and interests.

## Reflect on Your Childhood

THINK BACK TO activities or hobbies you enjoyed as a child. Childhood interests often provide clues about your natural inclinations and passions. Reflect on what brought you joy, sparked your curiosity, or made you lose track of time.

## Take Notice of Your Curiosity and Excitement

TAKE NOTE OF the things that pique your curiosity and ignite a sense of excitement within you. Pay attention to topics, activities, or experiences that captivate your attention and make you eager to learn more. Follow those interests and explore them further.

### Experiment and Explore

BE OPEN TO trying new activities and experiences. Step outside of your comfort zone and explore different hobbies, sports, arts, or subjects that you haven't tried before. Be willing to experiment and discover what resonates with you. Keep an open mind and embrace the process of exploration. This exploration can provide valuable insights and help you refine your understanding of what truly resonates with you.

### Identify Your Strengths

RECOGNIZE YOUR NATURAL strengths and talents. Reflect on the things that come naturally to you or that you excel at. Your passions are often intertwined with your strengths. Identify the activities or areas where you feel confident and enjoy using your abilities.

### Listen to Your Inner Voice

PAY ATTENTION TO your inner voice and intuition. Tune in to your gut feelings and inner desires. What does your heart long for? What excites and energizes you? Trust your instincts and listen to the inner guidance that leads you toward your passions and interests.

## Reflect on What Brings You Joy

CONSIDER THE ACTIVITIES or experiences that bring you a sense of joy and fulfillment. Reflect on the moments when you feel most alive and engaged. What activities make you lose track of time or bring a smile to your face? Follow those moments of joy to uncover your passions.

## Seek Inspiration

SURROUND YOURSELF WITH sources of inspiration. Read books, listen to podcasts, watch documentaries, or engage in conversations that expose you to new ideas and possibilities. Seek out role models or mentors who have pursued their passions and can inspire you to do the same.

## Embrace a Growth Mindset

ADOPT A GROWTH mindset that allows you to embrace challenges and view setbacks as opportunities for learning and growth. Understand that the journey of discovering your passions may involve trial and error. Embrace the process and see it as an adventure of self-discovery.

## Set Aside Dedicated Time

CREATE DEDICATED TIME for self-reflection and exploration. Set aside moments in your schedule to engage in activities that nourish your soul and allow you to explore different interests. Make it a priority to invest time in yourself and your journey of discovering your passions.

## Be Patient and Open-Minded

REMEMBER THAT DISCOVERING your passions and interests is a process that takes time. Be patient with yourself and open to the possibility that your passions may evolve or change over time. Allow yourself the freedom to explore, experiment, and grow along the way.

REMEMBER, DISCOVERING YOUR passions and interests is about connecting with your authentic self and finding fulfillment. Embrace the journey and trust that by following your curiosities and pursuing what brings you joy, you will uncover the passions that light up your life.

# ALIGNING YOUR ACTIONS WITH YOUR VALUES

ALIGNING YOUR ACTIONS with your values is an essential step toward living a fulfilling and purpose-driven life. When your actions are in harmony with your deeply held values, you experience a sense of integrity and authenticity. Here are some strategies to help you align your actions with your values.

## Identify Your Core Values

TAKE THE TIME to reflect on your core values, those principles and beliefs that are most important to you. Consider what truly matters to you in different areas of your life, such as relationships, work, health, and personal growth. Clarify your values and write them down.

## Prioritize Your Values

ONCE YOU HAVE identified your core values, prioritize them based on their significance in your life.

Determine which values are nonnegotiable and hold the greatest importance to you. This prioritization will guide your decision-making process and help you align your actions accordingly.

### Define What Each Value Means to You

GAIN A CLEAR understanding of what each value means to you personally. Define what it looks like to embody each value in your daily life. This clarity will serve as a compass for aligning your actions with your values and making decisions that resonate with your authentic self.

### Assess Your Current Actions

TAKE AN HONEST inventory of your current actions and behaviors. Evaluate whether they are in alignment with your values or if there are any inconsistencies. Identify any areas where you may be compromising or neglecting your values.

### Set Goals Aligned with Your Values

SET MEANINGFUL GOALS that align with your values. Determine what you want to achieve in different areas of your life while ensuring that these goals reflect your core values. Aligning your goals with your values provides a sense of purpose and motivates you to act in line with what truly matters to you.

### Practice Mindful Decision-Making

CULTIVATE MINDFULNESS IN your decision-making process. Before making choices or taking actions, pause and consider how they align with your values. Ask yourself if a particular decision or action is in alignment with what you truly value. Use your values as a guide to make choices that support your authentic self.

### Take Small Steps Toward Alignment

START BY MAKING small changes in your daily life that align with your values. Identify specific actions you can take that reflect your values and integrate them into your routine. These small steps gradually build a greater sense of alignment and integrity.

### Seek Out Accountability and Support

SHARE YOUR VALUES and intentions with trusted individuals who can hold you accountable. Surround yourself with people who also value and respect your principles. Seek support from others who are on a similar journey of aligning their actions with their values.

## Reflect and Learn from Setbacks

RECOGNIZE THAT ALIGNMENT with your values is an ongoing process. There may be times when you stumble or make choices that do not fully align with your values. Use these setbacks as opportunities for growth and self-reflection. Learn from them and adjust to realign with your values moving forward.

## Practice Self-Reflection

REGULARLY ENGAGE IN self-reflection to assess your alignment with your values. Set aside time to evaluate your actions, choices, and behaviors. Ask yourself if you are living in accordance with your values and if there are areas where you can further align your actions with what you truly value.

REMEMBER, ALIGNING YOUR actions with your values is a continual practice that requires self-awareness, intentionality, and self-compassion. By consciously living in accordance with your values, you create a life that is meaningful, fulfilling, and authentic to who you are.

## SETTING MEANINGFUL GOALS

SETTING MEANINGFUL GOALS is an important step toward creating a purposeful and fulfilling life. Meaningful goals align with your values, passions, and aspirations, providing direction and motivation to pursue what truly matters to you. Here are some strategies to help you set meaningful goals.

### Reflect on Your Values

BEGIN BY REFLECTING on your core values. Identify the principles and beliefs that are most important to you. Consider how these values can guide your goal-setting process and ensure that your goals align with what you truly value.

### Connect with Your Passions

EXPLORE YOUR PASSIONS and interests to gain a deeper understanding of what brings you joy and fulfillment. Reflect on the activities, subjects, or causes that ignite your enthusiasm and curiosity. Set goals that incorporate your passions to create a sense of purpose and motivation.

### Set SMART Goals

USE THE SMART goal framework to make your goals specific, measurable, attainable, relevant, and time-bound. Specific goals clarify what you want to achieve, while measurable goals provide a way to track your progress. Ensure your goals are attainable and relevant to your values and aspirations and set a timeline to create a sense of urgency.

### Focus on Both Short-Term and Long-Term Goals

SET GOALS THAT encompass both short-term and long-term aspirations. Short-term goals allow you to make progress and experience a sense of achievement in the near future, while long-term goals provide a broader vision and guide your overall direction in life.

### Break Goals into Actionable Steps

BREAK DOWN YOUR goals into smaller, actionable steps. This helps you create a clear roadmap and allows you to track your progress more effectively. Each step brings you closer to your desired outcome, making your goals more manageable and achievable.

### Make Goals Challenging Yet Realistic

STRIKE A BALANCE between setting challenging goals that push you outside your comfort zone and ensuring they are realistic and attainable. Stretch yourself to grow and learn, but also be mindful of setting goals that are within your capabilities and resources.

### Write Down Your Goals

WRITE DOWN YOUR goals to solidify your commitment and increase accountability. Keep them in a visible place as a reminder of what you are working toward. Consider creating a vision board or journaling about your goals to further reinforce your intentions.

### Regularly Review and Adjust Your Goals

REGULARLY REVIEW YOUR goals to assess your progress and make necessary adjustments. As circumstances and priorities change, your goals may need to be modified. Stay flexible and open to adapting your goals to align with your evolving aspirations.

## Celebrate Milestones and Progress

ACKNOWLEDGE AND CELEBRATE your achievements along the way. Celebrating milestones, no matter how small, reinforces your progress and motivates you to continue pursuing your goals. Use these moments of celebration to reflect on how far you've come and recommit to your journey.

REMEMBER, SETTING MEANINGFUL goals is a dynamic process that evolves over time. Stay connected to your values, passions, and aspirations as you set and pursue your goals. By setting meaningful goals, you create a road map for a purpose-driven life that brings you fulfillment, growth, and a sense of accomplishment.

# CREATING A PERSONAL MISSION STATEMENT

A PERSONAL MISSION statement is a concise statement that captures your core purpose, values, and aspirations. It serves as a guiding principle for your actions, decisions, and overall direction in life. Before you begin crafting your personal mission statement, you'll once again reflect on your values to ensure that the principles and beliefs most important to you help guide this process. Here are some steps to help you create your personal mission statement.

## Identify Your Passions and Strengths

EXPLORE YOUR PASSIONS, interests, and talents. Reflect on the activities and pursuits that bring you joy, energize you, and allow you to express your unique strengths. Your mission statement should incorporate your passions and leverage your strengths.

## Define Your Purpose

CLARIFY YOUR PURPOSE or overarching goal in life. Ask yourself what you want to contribute to the world, what impact you want to make, and what legacy you want to leave behind. Consider how your unique abilities and passions align with a larger purpose.

## Reflect on Your Impact

CONSIDER THE WAYS in which you want to make a difference in the world. Reflect on the kind of impact you want to have on individuals, communities, or society. Visualize the positive change you aspire to create and how it aligns with your passions, values, and strengths.

## Write a Draft

BEGIN WRITING A draft of your mission statement. Start with a concise statement that encapsulates your purpose and values. Use clear and inspiring language to convey the essence of who you are and what you aspire to achieve. Don't worry about getting it perfect in the first draft—just let your thoughts flow.

## Refine and Iterate

REFINE YOUR MISSION statement by reviewing and revising your initial draft. Seek clarity, simplicity, and alignment with your values and aspirations. Remove any unnecessary or vague language and ensure that your statement resonates with your authentic self.

## Seek Feedback

SHARE YOUR MISSION statement with trusted friends, family, or mentors who know you well. Seek their feedback and insights to gain different perspectives. Consider their input while staying true to your own beliefs and values. Use the feedback to refine and improve your statement.

## Make It Personal and Specific

TAILOR YOUR MISSION statement to reflect your individuality and unique journey. Avoid generic statements and make it personal by incorporating your own experiences, passions, and values. The more specific and authentic it is to you, the more meaningful it becomes.

### Use Powerful Language

CHOOSE POWERFUL AND inspiring language that reflects your values, passions, and aspirations. Use words that evoke emotion and create a sense of purpose and motivation. Be intentional with your choice of words to make your mission statement impactful.

### Keep It Concise

AIM TO KEEP your mission statement concise and to the point. A few sentences or a short paragraph can effectively capture the essence of your mission. Avoid excessive details and focus on communicating the core message.

### Revisit and Reconnect

REGULARLY REVISIT YOUR mission statement to ensure it remains relevant and aligned with your evolving values and aspirations. Use it as a touchstone to guide your decisions and actions. Reconnect with the purpose and inspiration it provides in your life.

REMEMBER, YOUR PERSONAL mission statement reflects your authentic self and serves as a compass for living a purposeful and meaningful life. It can evolve over time as you gain new insights and experiences. Embrace the process of creating your mission statement and let it inspire and guide you on your journey of personal growth and fulfillment.

# FIVE

# NURTURING RELATIONSHIPS

*"Our rewards in life will always be in exact proportion to the amount of consideration we show toward others."*

—EARL NIGHTINGALE

IN THE HEART of a bustling metropolis, amidst the towering skyscrapers and bustling crowds, there lived a woman named Sarah. She was a high-powered executive navigating the concrete jungle with impeccable professionalism. But as the city's ceaseless rhythm continued, Sarah often found herself yearning for something more.

In the day-to-day course of her demanding job, Sarah had become somewhat of a recluse, her daily life consumed by meetings, deadlines, and a constant stream of emails. It was not unusual for her to leave the office late into the night only to return early the next morning. Over time, the city's relentless pace began to take a toll on her sense of well-being.

One evening after a particularly grueling day at work, Sarah decided to take a walk through a nearby park. She had always found solace in nature and knew that this small respite could provide the connection she had been craving.

As she strolled through the park, the scent of blooming flowers and the sound of rustling leaves enveloped her. The gentle breeze on her face and the soft chirping of birds made her feel alive in a way she hadn't felt in years. It was in this serene moment that Sarah began to realize the importance of being connected, not just to her job but to the world around her and the people who inhabited it.

In the following weeks, Sarah made a conscious effort to build and maintain meaningful relationships with those around her. She started by reconnecting with old friends she had lost touch with and found herself immersed in conversations that brought back a sense of nostalgia and joy. She also took the time to get to know her coworkers on a personal level, discovering that beneath their professional facades, they too were yearning for genuine connections.

One sunny weekend, Sarah decided to volunteer at a local community center, where she met a diverse group of people who were united by a shared purpose: to make their neighborhood a better place. Through their collective efforts, they created a sense of belonging and community that was both heartwarming and fulfilling.

As the months passed, Sarah's transformation was evident to those who knew her. She no longer viewed the city as an overwhelming, lonely place but as a vibrant community of people who, like her, sought connections, support, and a sense of belonging.

Her journey of self-discovery led her to prioritize her well-being and happiness. She continued to excel in her career, but she now understood that success was not solely measured by professional achievements. The fundamental human need for connection played a crucial role in her overall well-being.

Sarah's life was a testament to the importance of being connected in a bustling city. She realized that building and maintaining meaningful relationships with others and fostering a sense of belonging and community were not just desires but also essential aspects of a fulfilling life. In the end, she had not just discovered a better work-life balance—she had discovered a profound sense of happiness and fulfillment in the connections she had forged.

# THE IMPORTANCE OF CONNECTION

CONNECTION IS A fundamental human need that plays a crucial role in our overall well-being and happiness. It involves building and maintaining meaningful relationships with others as well as fostering a sense of belonging and community. Here are some key aspects highlighting the importance of connection.

## Emotional Support

CONNECTION PROVIDES US with emotional support during challenging times. Having trusted individuals in our lives who can offer understanding, empathy, and encouragement can help us navigate difficulties and cope with stress more effectively.

## Mental and Emotional Well-being

MEANINGFUL CONNECTIONS CONTRIBUTE to our mental and emotional well-being. Engaging in positive social interactions releases hormones like oxytocin, which promotes feelings of happiness, reduces stress, and enhances overall emotional resilience.

### Sense of Belonging

CONNECTION GIVES US a sense of belonging and acceptance. It helps us feel valued, understood, and part of something greater than ourselves. This sense of belonging fosters a deeper sense of purpose and meaning in life.

### Increased Empathy and Understanding

CONNECTION ALLOWS US to empathize with others and gain a better understanding of diverse perspectives. By engaging in open and meaningful conversations, we expand our knowledge, challenge our biases, and develop a broader worldview.

### Physical Health Benefits

STRONG SOCIAL CONNECTIONS have been linked to improved physical health. Studies have shown that individuals with robust social support networks tend to have lower rates of chronic illnesses, faster recovery from illnesses, and increased longevity.

## Personal Growth and Learning

CONNECTION PROVIDES OPPORTUNITIES for personal growth and learning through the exchange of ideas, experiences, and knowledge. Interacting with others who have different backgrounds and viewpoints exposes us to new perspectives, promotes critical thinking, and fosters personal development.

## Boosted Resilience

CONNECTED INDIVIDUALS OFTEN display higher levels of resilience in the face of adversity. The support and encouragement from their social connections help them bounce back from setbacks, overcome challenges, and adapt more effectively to change.

## Opportunities for Collaboration

CONNECTION OPENS DOORS to collaborative opportunities. By building connections with others who share similar interests or goals, we can collaborate, share resources, and work together to achieve common objectives.

## Enhanced Happiness

MEANINGFUL CONNECTIONS CONTRIBUTE to overall happiness and life satisfaction. The joy and fulfillment that come from nurturing and maintaining relationships are essential for our emotional well-being.

### Social Engagement and Fun

CONNECTION FACILITATES SOCIAL engagement and the opportunity to engage in enjoyable activities with others. Participating in social events, sharing hobbies, and spending quality time with loved ones enhances our overall happiness and creates lasting memories.

IN TODAY'S INCREASINGLY digital world, it is important to prioritize and nurture our connections. Making time for face-to-face interactions, active listening, and genuine engagement can strengthen our relationships and foster deeper connections. By valuing and investing in connection, we enhance our well-being and create a more fulfilling and meaningful life.

# BUILDING HEALTHY AND MEANINGFUL RELATIONSHIPS

HEALTHY AND MEANINGFUL relationships are essential for our overall well-being, happiness, and personal growth. They provide support, connection, and a sense of belonging. Here are some key principles and practices for building and nurturing healthy and meaningful relationships.

## Communication

EFFECTIVE COMMUNICATION IS the foundation of any healthy relationship. Be open, honest, and transparent in your communication. Listen actively, validate the other person's feelings, and express your own thoughts and emotions with respect and clarity.

## Trust and Honesty

TRUST IS THE cornerstone of strong relationships. Foster trust by being reliable, keeping your word, and maintaining confidentiality. Be honest and authentic in your interactions and avoid deceit or manipulation.

## Mutual Respect

TREAT OTHERS WITH respect and dignity, honoring their boundaries, opinions, and values. Practice active empathy and seek to understand their perspectives without judgment. Respect their autonomy and individuality.

## Emotional Support

OFFER EMOTIONAL SUPPORT and be available for others when they need someone to lean on. Show empathy, compassion, and understanding. Validate their feelings and provide a safe space for them to express themselves.

## Quality Time

INVEST TIME AND energy in building meaningful connections. Create opportunities for quality time with loved ones. Engage in activities together, share experiences, and create memories. Prioritize presence and attentive listening during these moments.

## Personal Boundaries

ESTABLISH AND RESPECT healthy boundaries in your relationships. Clearly communicate your own boundaries and be mindful of others' boundaries.

Respect each other's needs for personal space, privacy, and individuality.

### Forgiveness and Conflict Resolution

UNDERSTAND THAT CONFLICTS are a natural part of relationships. Practice forgiveness and seek resolution through open and respectful dialogue. Focus on finding common ground and working together to overcome challenges.

### Appreciation and Gratitude

EXPRESS APPRECIATION AND gratitude for the people in your life. Recognize and acknowledge their contributions, efforts, and positive qualities. Regularly express your gratitude and let them know how much they mean to you.

### Support for Personal Growth

ENCOURAGE PERSONAL GROWTH and development in your relationships. Support each other's goals, dreams, and aspirations. Provide encouragement, constructive feedback, and a nurturing environment for individual growth.

## Empathy and Understanding

CULTIVATE EMPATHY BY putting yourself in the other person's shoes and seeking to understand their experiences and perspectives. Be curious and open-minded. Practice active listening and strive to understand their feelings and needs.

## Healthy Conflict Resolution

WHEN CONFLICTS ARISE, approach them with a solution-oriented mindset. Focus on active listening, finding common ground, and seeking mutually beneficial resolutions. Avoid blame, defensiveness, and destructive communication patterns.

## Showing Up Authentically

BE YOURSELF IN your relationships. Embrace vulnerability and show up authentically, allowing others to see the real you. Share your thoughts, feelings, and experiences honestly to foster a deeper connection.

## Celebrating Differences

EMBRACE AND CELEBRATE the differences between you and others. Recognize that diversity in thoughts, perspectives, and backgrounds can enrich your relationships and bring new insights and growth.

## Regular Check-Ins

MAKE AN EFFORT to regularly check in with the people in your life. Ask about their well-being, listen attentively, and offer support when needed. Regularly express your care and concern for them.

REMEMBER, BUILDING HEALTHY and meaningful relationships takes time, effort, and commitment from all parties involved. It requires ongoing communication, empathy, and mutual respect. By investing in these practices, you can cultivate strong, fulfilling, and long-lasting relationships that contribute to your overall well-being and happiness.

# EFFECTIVE COMMUNICATION AND ACTIVE LISTENING

EFFECTIVE COMMUNICATION AND active listening are vital skills for building strong relationships and fostering understanding. They promote clarity, connection, and mutual respect in interactions with others. Here are some key principles and practices for effective communication and active listening.

## Be Present

BE FULLY PRESENT and engaged in your conversations. Minimize distractions and give your undivided attention to the speaker. Show genuine interest and create a safe space for open dialogue.

## Choose the Right Time and Place

CONSIDER THE TIMING and environment for effective communication. Find a suitable setting where both parties can focus and feel comfortable. Avoid distractions and interruptions as much as possible.

## Use Clear and Concise Language

EXPRESS YOUR THOUGHTS and ideas clearly and concisely. Use language that is easily understood by the listener. Avoid jargon or complex terminology unless it is appropriate for the context.

## Practice Active Listening

ACTIVELY LISTEN TO the speaker by giving your full attention and demonstrating interest. Maintain eye contact, nod, and provide verbal or nonverbal cues to show that you are engaged. Avoid interrupting and allow the speaker to express themselves fully.

## Seek Understanding

STRIVE TO UNDERSTAND the speaker's perspective and feelings. Put yourself in their shoes and try to see things from their point of view. Ask clarifying questions to ensure comprehension and demonstrate your interest in their thoughts.

## Validate and Empathize

VALIDATE THE SPEAKER'S emotions and experiences. Show empathy by acknowledging their feelings and demonstrating that you understand their perspective. Avoid dismissing or belittling their emotions.

## Note Nonverbal Communication

PAY ATTENTION TO nonverbal cues such as body language, facial expressions, and tone of voice. These cues provide additional context and can help you understand the speaker's emotions and intentions. Be mindful of your own nonverbal cues as well.

## Utilize Reflective Responses

REFLECT ON WHAT the speaker has said to confirm your understanding. Summarize or paraphrase their main points to ensure clarity and demonstrate that you are actively listening. This also allows the speaker to correct any misconceptions.

## Be Open to Feedback

BE RECEPTIVE TO feedback and constructive criticism. Listen attentively without becoming defensive. Consider the other person's perspective and be willing to learn and grow from their input.

## Practice Patience

BE PATIENT DURING conversations, especially when discussing sensitive or challenging topics. Allow the speaker enough time to express themselves fully and avoid rushing to respond. Patience fosters a safe and supportive environment for open communication.

### Choose Your Words Wisely

BE MINDFUL OF the words you use and how they may be interpreted by the listener. Use respectful and nonjudgmental language. Avoid using inflammatory or derogatory language that can hinder productive communication.

### Be Respectful

TREAT OTHERS WITH respect and kindness in your communication. Avoid interrupting, talking over others, or dismissing their ideas. Create an atmosphere of mutual respect and equal participation.

### Provide Feedback

PROVIDE CONSTRUCTIVE FEEDBACK in a thoughtful and considerate manner. Use "I" statements to express your observations and feelings without blaming or criticizing the other person. Be specific and focus on behavior or actions rather than personal attacks.

## Follow Up

AFTER A CONVERSATION, follow up with the other person to ensure understanding and address any lingering concerns or questions. This shows your commitment to effective communication and maintaining the relationship.

REMEMBER, EFFECTIVE COMMUNICATION and active listening require practice and ongoing effort. By cultivating these skills, you can foster meaningful connections, resolve conflicts, and promote understanding in your relationships and interactions with others.

## RESOLVING CONFLICTS WITH COMPASSION

CONFLICT IS A natural part of human interactions, but resolving conflicts with compassion can lead to more positive outcomes and stronger relationships. When approaching conflict resolution with compassion, consider the following principles and practices.

### Demonstrate Empathy

EMPATHY IS A key component of resolving conflicts with compassion. Seek to understand the other person's perspective, feelings, and needs. Put yourself in their shoes and imagine how they might be experiencing the situation.

### Practice Active Listening

PRACTICE ACTIVE LISTENING during conflict resolution. Give your full attention to the other person, allowing them to express their thoughts and emotions without interruption. Show genuine interest and reflect on what they've said to ensure understanding.

### Utilize Nondefensive Communication

AVOID BECOMING DEFENSIVE or reactive during conflicts. Instead, focus on maintaining an open and calm demeanor. Respond with empathy and understanding, even if the other person's words or actions have triggered negative emotions.

### Validate Emotions

RECOGNIZE AND VALIDATE the emotions of both you and the other person involved in the conflict. Emotions are often at the core of conflicts, and acknowledging them can help create a sense of safety and understanding.

### Seek Common Ground

LOOK FOR AREAS of agreement or shared interests to build upon. Identify common goals or objectives that both parties can work toward. This can help create a sense of collaboration and foster a cooperative mindset.

## Practice Self-Reflection

TAKE TIME TO reflect on your own role in the conflict. Be willing to acknowledge any mistakes or areas where you could have contributed to the conflict. This self-awareness allows for personal growth and helps create a more compassionate approach to conflict resolution.

## Use "I" Statements

WHEN EXPRESSING YOUR thoughts and feelings during conflict resolution, use "I" statements to avoid sounding accusatory or placing blame. Focus on expressing your own experiences and needs without attacking the other person.

## Employ a Problem-Solving Approach

SHIFT THE FOCUS from blame to problem-solving. Collaboratively explore potential solutions and alternatives. Brainstorm together and encourage open dialogue to find a resolution that addresses the needs of both parties.

## Exercise Patience and Tolerance

CONFLICT RESOLUTION CAN take time and may require patience. Be willing to give the process the necessary time and space it needs. Practice tolerance by remaining open-minded and respectful even when faced with differing opinions or perspectives.

### Discover Win-Win Solutions

STRIVE FOR WIN-WIN outcomes where both parties feel their needs and concerns have been addressed. Look for creative solutions that can meet the underlying interests of both sides.

### Use Compassionate Language

CHOOSE YOUR WORDS carefully, using language that is compassionate, respectful, and nonconfrontational. Avoid harsh or derogatory language that can escalate tensions. Speak with kindness and empathy even when expressing differing viewpoints.

### Seek Mediation If Needed

IN SITUATIONS WHERE resolving conflicts directly becomes challenging, consider involving a neutral third party as a mediator. A mediator can facilitate communication, ensure fairness, and help both parties find common ground.

## Focus on Relationship Building

CONFLICT RESOLUTION PROVIDES an opportunity to strengthen relationships. Use the process as a chance to deepen understanding, foster empathy, and build trust. Prioritize the long-term relationship over short-term disagreements.

## Practice Forgiveness

AS CONFLICTS ARE resolved, practice forgiveness and let go of any lingering resentment or anger. Holding onto grudges can hinder the healing process and strain relationships. Instead, focus on moving forward with compassion and understanding.

REMEMBER, RESOLVING CONFLICTS with compassion takes practice and effort. By approaching conflicts with empathy, active listening, and a willingness to find mutually beneficial solutions, you can foster understanding, strengthen relationships, and promote a harmonious environment.

SIX

# SELF-CARE AND WELL-BEING

*"Never bend your head. Always hold it high. Look the world straight in the face."*

—*HELEN KELLER*

IN THE HEART of a bustling city, there lived a man named Ethan. He was a dedicated software engineer known for his unwavering commitment to his work. Every morning, he would rush to the office, and his nights often extended well into the wee hours as he tackled complex coding challenges. His coworkers admired his dedication, but they couldn't help but notice the toll it was taking on him.

Ethan's life was a whirlwind of deadlines and meetings, and it seemed like the demands of the fast-paced tech world never relented. He was constantly juggling multiple projects, leaving him with little time for rest or relaxation. His weekends often slipped away in a haze of more coding, and his social life dwindled to a mere shadow of what it once was.

One particularly hectic day, as the city bustled with honking cars and bustling pedestrians, Ethan found himself exhausted and overwhelmed. His eyes felt heavy, and a persistent headache throbbed in the back of his skull. He knew he was on the brink of burnout.

That evening, while scrolling through his emails, Ethan received a message from his best friend Sophia. She had been worried about him and suggested they meet up for dinner. It was the first time in weeks that he'd seen an invitation from someone other than his colleagues or clients.

As Ethan sat across from Sophia at a cozy bistro, he realized the importance of prioritizing self-care. Her laughter, her stories, and the genuine connection they shared reminded him of what he had been missing. He confided in Sophia about the immense stress he'd been under, and she listened with empathy.

"Life is a marathon, not a sprint, Ethan," she said. "You have to take care of yourself to keep running. Your work is important, but so is your well-being."

Over the course of their meal, Sophia convinced Ethan to take a step back from work, even if just for a weekend. She shared her own experiences of burnout and the necessity of creating a balance between work and self-care.

The following weekend, Ethan heeded Sophia's advice and decided to step away from his computer. He spent his Saturday at a local park, surrounded by the soothing sounds of nature. He even picked up a novel he had been meaning to read for months and took leisurely strolls without checking his work email.

The time away allowed Ethan to rejuvenate and recharge. He returned to work on Monday with renewed energy and a clearer perspective. He began to set boundaries, dedicating time to self-care, exercise, and socializing. It wasn't long before he found that he could still excel at his job while maintaining a healthier work-life balance.

Ethan's journey was a lesson to himself and those around him about the crucial need to prioritize self-care in a demanding world. The bustling city remained a constant, but he had learned that within its frenetic rhythm, he could find moments of peace and balance. The path to well-being, he discovered, began with valuing and nurturing oneself, for it was only by taking care of himself that he could truly excel and prevent burnout in the long run.

## PRIORITIZING SELF-CARE IN A BUSY WORLD

IN A BUSY and demanding world, it's crucial to prioritize self-care to maintain your well-being and prevent burnout. Here are some principles and practices for prioritizing self-care.

### Recognize the Importance of Self-Care

UNDERSTAND THAT SELF-CARE is not selfish but necessary for your overall health and happiness. Recognize that taking care of yourself enables you to better care for others and fulfill your responsibilities more effectively.

### Assess Your Needs

TAKE TIME TO assess your physical, mental, and emotional needs. Reflect on what brings you joy, relaxation, and rejuvenation. Identify activities, practices, and habits that support your well-being.

## Set Boundaries

ESTABLISH CLEAR BOUNDARIES to protect your time and energy. Learn to say no to commitments that overwhelm you or do not align with your priorities. Communicate your limits to others and advocate for your own needs.

## Prioritize Time for Self-Care

SCHEDULE REGULAR TIME for self-care in your daily or weekly routine. Treat it as a nonnegotiable appointment with yourself. Whether it's a few minutes or several hours, carve out dedicated time for activities that recharge and nourish you.

## Practice Mindfulness

CULTIVATE MINDFULNESS BY staying present and fully engaged in the present moment. This helps you notice and attend to your needs, manage stress, and appreciate the small joys in life. Incorporate mindfulness into daily activities such as eating, walking, or taking breaks.

## Nurture Your Physical Well-Being

TAKE CARE OF your physical health through regular exercise, nutritious eating, and adequate sleep.

Prioritize activities that promote physical well-being, such as engaging in physical activity you enjoy or preparing nourishing meals.

### Engage in Activities That Bring You Joy

MAKE TIME FOR activities that bring you joy and fulfillment. Engage in hobbies, creative pursuits, or leisure activities that you find personally rewarding. These activities provide an outlet for self-expression and help you recharge.

### Practice Relaxation Techniques

INCORPORATE RELAXATION TECHNIQUES into your routine, such as deep breathing exercises, meditation, yoga, or mindfulness practices. These activities promote relaxation, stress reduction, and mental clarity.

### Seek Social Support

CULTIVATE MEANINGFUL CONNECTIONS with others. Surround yourself with supportive and positive people who uplift you. Engage in social activities that nourish your relationships and foster a sense of belonging.

### Exercise Self-Compassion

BE KIND AND compassionate to yourself. Acknowledge your limitations, imperfections, and mistakes without self-judgment. Treat yourself with the same kindness and understanding you would offer to a close friend.

### Unplug and Disconnect

TAKE REGULAR BREAKS from technology and digital devices. Disconnect from work emails, social media, and constant notifications. Allow yourself time for quiet reflection, relaxation, and being present in the moment.

### Create Healthy Routines

ESTABLISH HEALTHY ROUTINES that support your self-care goals. Prioritize regular exercise, consistent sleep patterns, and balanced meals. Incorporate self-care activities into your daily routine, such as taking breaks, practicing gratitude, or engaging in hobbies.

### Practice Stress Management

DEVELOP STRATEGIES TO manage stress effectively. This may include deep breathing exercises, journaling, seeking support from a therapist or counselor, or engaging in stress-reducing activities such as nature walks or listening to calming music.

### Create Daily Rituals for Self-Renewal

DAILY RITUALS CAN be powerful tools for self-renewal and rejuvenation. They provide a consistent and intentional way to prioritize self-care and nourish your mind, body, and spirit. Revisit practices and exercises in gratitude and mindfulness for some ideas on daily routines that serve as excellent self-care rituals.

### Regularly Assess and Adjust

CONTINUOUSLY ASSESS YOUR self-care practices and adjust as needed. Your needs may change over time, so be flexible and responsive to what serves you best in different seasons of life.

REMEMBER, PRIORITIZING SELF-CARE is an ongoing process and requires conscious effort. By making self-care a priority, you can maintain your well-being, increase your resilience, and cultivate a more balanced and fulfilling life.

# NURTURING YOUR PHYSICAL, MENTAL, AND EMOTIONAL WELL-BEING

TAKING CARE OF your overall well-being involves nurturing your physical, mental, and emotional health. Here are some practices to help you nurture each aspect.

## PHYSICAL WELL-BEING

### Regular Exercise

ENGAGE IN REGULAR physical activity that you enjoy. It can be as simple as walking, jogging, cycling, or participating in sports. Find activities that fit your lifestyle and make them a regular part of your routine.

### Balanced Nutrition

EAT A WELL-BALANCED diet that includes a variety of fruits, vegetables, whole grains, lean proteins, and healthy fats. Stay hydrated by drinking enough water throughout the day. Limit processed foods, sugary drinks, and excessive alcohol consumption.

### Adequate Sleep

PRIORITIZE QUALITY SLEEP by maintaining a consistent sleep schedule and creating a calming bedtime routine. Aim for seven to nine hours of sleep per night to support your physical and mental well-being.

## Regular Check-Ups

SCHEDULE ROUTINE CHECK-UPS with your healthcare provider for preventive care and early detection of any health issues. Stay up to date with vaccinations and screenings appropriate for your age and gender.

## Relaxation and Rest

INCORPORATE RELAXATION TECHNIQUES into your routine, such as deep breathing exercises, meditation, or practicing mindfulness. Take breaks throughout the day to recharge and allow yourself time for rest and rejuvenation.

# MENTAL WELL-BEING

## Self-Care Practices

ENGAGE IN ACTIVITIES that promote mental well-being, such as reading, listening to music, practicing hobbies, or spending time in nature. Find activities that help you relax, unwind, and recharge your mental energy.

## Stress Management

DEVELOP EFFECTIVE STRESS management strategies that work for you. This may include exercise, practicing mindfulness, journaling, talking to a trusted friend or therapist, or engaging in activities that help you reduce stress.

## Cognitive Stimulation

KEEP YOUR MIND active and engaged by challenging yourself intellectually. Engage in activities such as reading, puzzles, learning a new skill, or pursuing hobbies that stimulate your cognitive abilities.

## Emotional Expression

ALLOW YOURSELF TO express and process your emotions in a healthy way. Practice self-reflection, journaling, or talking to a supportive friend or therapist about your feelings. Engaging in creative outlets, such as art or music, can also help with emotional expression.

## Positive Mindset

CULTIVATE A POSITIVE mindset by focusing on gratitude, practicing self-compassion, and reframing negative thoughts. Surround yourself with positive influences and practice optimism to enhance your mental well-being.

# EMOTIONAL WELL-BEING

## Emotional Awareness

DEVELOP SELF-AWARENESS OF your emotions and their underlying causes. Pay attention to your feelings without judgment and seek to understand their triggers and impact on your well-being.

## Emotional Regulation

LEARN HEALTHY STRATEGIES to regulate your emotions when faced with challenges or stress. This may include deep breathing exercises, mindfulness practices, seeking support from loved ones, or engaging in activities that bring you joy and peace.

## Social Connections

NURTURE MEANINGFUL RELATIONSHIPS with supportive and caring individuals. Spend time with loved ones, engage in activities together, and foster connections that provide emotional support and a sense of belonging.

## Boundaries

SET CLEAR BOUNDARIES in your relationships to protect your emotional well-being. Learn to say no when necessary, communicate your needs assertively, and prioritize self-care to maintain healthy emotional boundaries.

## Seek Help When Needed

IF YOU'RE EXPERIENCING persistent emotional difficulties or mental health challenges, seek support from a mental health professional. They can provide guidance, support, and therapeutic interventions to help you navigate and overcome emotional struggles.

REMEMBER THAT NURTURING your physical, mental, and emotional well-being is an ongoing process. It requires self-awareness, commitment, and the willingness to prioritize self-care in your daily life. By taking proactive steps to care for yourself, you can enhance your overall well-being and lead a more balanced and fulfilling life.

## FINDING BALANCE AND SETTING BOUNDARIES

IN TODAY'S FAST-PACED and demanding world, finding balance and setting boundaries is essential for your well-being. It allows you to prioritize your needs, manage your time and energy effectively, and maintain a healthy equilibrium in various aspects of your life. Prioritizing self-care and staying clear on your personal values and priorities will go a long way here. Here are some more strategies to help you find balance and set boundaries.

### Learn to Say No

PRACTICE SAYING NO to commitments, activities, or requests that do not align with your values or overwhelm your schedule. It's okay to decline politely and prioritize your well-being. Saying no allows you to create space for what truly matters to you.

### Set Clear Boundaries

ESTABLISH CLEAR BOUNDARIES with others regarding your time, energy, and personal space. Communicate your boundaries assertively and respectfully. This can involve setting limits on work hours, responding to emails outside of designated times, or carving out personal time without interruptions.

### Delegate and Ask for Help

RECOGNIZE THAT YOU don't have to do everything alone. Delegate tasks when possible and ask for help when needed. Delegating responsibilities can free up time and energy, allowing you to focus on what matters most to you.

### Practice Time Management

DEVELOP EFFECTIVE TIME management skills to allocate your time wisely. Prioritize tasks based on their importance and urgency. Use tools such as to-do lists, calendars, or productivity apps to help you stay organized and focused.

### Create Boundaries with Technology

SET BOUNDARIES WITH technology to prevent it from encroaching on your personal time and well-being. Establish tech-free zones or specific time periods where you disconnect from devices and focus on other aspects of your life.

### Assess and Adjust Regularly

REGULARLY ASSESS YOUR commitments, routines, and boundaries to ensure they align with your current needs and priorities. Be willing to make adjustments as circumstances change. Flexibility and adaptability are key to maintaining balance.

### Practice Mindfulness

UTILIZE MINDFULNESS PRACTICES in your daily life to stay present and aware of your thoughts, emotions, and physical sensations. Mindfulness helps you tune into your needs and make conscious choices that support balance and well-being.

### Seek Support and Accountability

SURROUND YOURSELF WITH a supportive network of friends, family, or mentors who understand the importance of balance and boundaries. Share your goals and challenges with them, and ask for their support and accountability in maintaining balance.

### Learn to Manage Guilt

LET GO OF guilt when setting boundaries or taking time for yourself. Understand that taking care of your needs is not selfish but necessary for your overall well-being. Practice self-compassion and remind yourself that you deserve balance and self-care.

### Embrace Flexibility

BALANCE IS NOT about rigidly dividing your time equally among all areas of your life; it's about being flexible and adjusting based on your priorities and circumstances. Embrace the ebb and flow of life while maintaining a general sense of equilibrium.

REMEMBER, FINDING BALANCE and setting boundaries is an ongoing process. It requires self-awareness, self-compassion, and consistent practice. By prioritizing your well-being and creating healthy boundaries, you can lead a more balanced and fulfilling life.

SEVEN

# EMBRACING CHANGE AND RESILIENCE

*"Life isn't about waiting for the storm to pass. It's about learning how to dance in the rain."*

VIVIAN GREENE

IN A BUSTLING city, there lived a woman named Emily who was known for her thriving marketing career. She had always been comfortable in her routine, with her days meticulously planned and her professional life well-established. But change, as it often does, came knocking on her door.

One day, Emily received the news that her company was undergoing a major restructuring. Her comfortable position would no longer exist, and she was faced with two choices: to resist change or to embrace it as an opportunity for growth. After careful consideration, she chose the latter.

Embracing change meant leaving behind the familiarity of her old role and diving into the uncertainty of a new one. It was a challenge that excited her but also brought a wave of apprehension. Nevertheless, she recognized that change was an inevitable part of life, and she was determined to make the most of it.

As she transitioned into her new role, Emily faced a steep learning curve. She had to acquire new skills, adapt to a different work environment, and build relationships with a whole new team. The change was demanding, but Emily approached it with an open mind and a willingness to learn.

In this process, she discovered her own resilience and adaptability. She found that embracing change had pushed her beyond her comfort zone and had opened a world of opportunities for personal and professional development. With each new challenge, she learned, grew, and became more capable than she had ever imagined.

Emily's colleagues noticed her dedication and her commitment to making the best of the change. She became a source of inspiration to them, showing that change could be a catalyst for personal and professional growth. Her positive attitude and adaptability were contagious, and the entire team began to view change as an opportunity rather than a threat.

Over time, Emily not only excelled in her new role but also rose through the ranks, earning her a leadership position. Her journey of embracing change had not only led to personal growth but also professional success. She realized that the changes in her career had propelled her to new heights far beyond what her previous comfort zone could have offered.

Emily's story became a testament to the idea that change is an inevitable part of life. By embracing it as an opportunity for growth, both personally and professionally, she had not just survived the transition but also thrived in it. She had transformed change from something to be feared into something to be welcomed, a force that could lead to greater achievements and personal development.

# EMBRACING CHANGE AS AN OPPORTUNITY FOR GROWTH

CHANGE IS AN inevitable part of life. Embracing it as an opportunity for growth can lead to personal and professional development. As always, as you learn to embrace change, it is important to maintain a mindset of growth and positivity and to see change as not an inconvenience, but as an opportunity for learning and adaptation. Here are some ways to embrace change and use it as a catalyst for growth.

## Embrace Discomfort

RECOGNIZE THAT GROWTH often occurs outside of your comfort zone. Be willing to step into the unknown and embrace the discomfort that comes with change. This willingness to explore unfamiliar territory can lead to personal transformation.

## Embrace Curiosity and Practice Adaptability

APPROACH CHANGE WITH curiosity and a desire to explore new possibilities. Ask questions, seek different perspectives, and be open to new ideas. Confronting change with curiosity and willingness to explore and learn will help you adapt to new situations and circumstances. Be open to different perspectives and approaches. See change as a chance to broaden your horizons and develop new skills.

### Seek Opportunities for Learning

VIEW CHANGE AS an opportunity to learn and acquire new knowledge or skills. Look for training programs, workshops, or courses that can help you develop the necessary competencies to navigate the changing landscape.

### Practice Self-Reflection

TAKE TIME FOR self-reflection during periods of change. Assess your strengths, weaknesses, and areas for growth. Reflect on how the change can help you develop new skills, broaden your experiences, or gain new insights about yourself.

### Build a Support Network

SURROUND YOURSELF WITH a supportive network of individuals who can provide guidance, encouragement, and mentorship during times of change. Share your experiences and seek their insights. Together, you can navigate change more effectively.

### Exercise Self-Compassion and Care

BE KIND AND patient with yourself as you navigate change. Acknowledge that growth takes time and that setbacks are a natural part of the process. Treat yourself with compassion and celebrate your progress along the way. Engage in activities that nurture your physical, mental, and emotional health, such as exercise, adequate sleep, healthy eating, and stress reduction techniques like meditation or deep breathing. Taking care of your mind, body, and spirit equips you with the energy and resilience needed to face challenges.

### Develop Problem-Solving Skills

ENHANCE YOUR PROBLEM-SOLVING skills to effectively tackle challenges. Break down problems into manageable steps, analyze potential solutions, and act. Developing problem-solving skills helps you approach difficulties with a proactive mindset and find effective solutions.

## Practice Emotional Regulation

LEARN TO MANAGE and regulate your emotions during difficult times. Recognize and acknowledge your emotions without letting them overwhelm you. Develop healthy coping mechanisms such as journaling, talking to a trusted confidant, or engaging in activities that bring you joy and relaxation.

## Celebrate Your Progress

TAKE TIME TO acknowledge and celebrate your growth along the journey. Recognize the milestones you've reached and the challenges you've overcome. Celebrating your progress reinforces your ability to adapt and thrive in the face of change.

## Seek Professional Support If Needed

IF YOU FIND yourself struggling to cope with challenges or experiencing persistent stress or emotional difficulties, don't hesitate to seek professional support. Therapists or counselors can provide guidance, support, and tools to enhance your resilience and well-being.

BY EMBRACING CHANGE as an opportunity for growth, you can develop resilience, expand your skills and experiences, and uncover new possibilities. Embracing change with a growth mindset allows you to evolve and thrive in an ever-changing world.

## CULTIVATING A POSITIVE MINDSET AROUND CHANGE

A POSITIVE MINDSET can significantly impact your overall well-being, resilience, and ability to navigate challenges. It involves adopting a positive outlook, focusing on the good in life, and reframing negative situations. Here are some strategies to cultivate a positive mindset.

### Focus on Solutions

INSTEAD OF DWELLING on problems, shift your focus to finding solutions. Approach challenges with a problem-solving mindset and actively seek ways to overcome obstacles. By focusing on solutions, you maintain a positive mindset and empower yourself to act.

### Visualize Success

USE THE POWER of visualization to imagine yourself succeeding and overcoming obstacles. Create a mental image of your desired outcome and visualize yourself confidently navigating challenges. Visualization can help reinforce a positive mindset and build confidence in your abilities.

**Surround Yourself with Positive Affirmations**

USE POSITIVE AFFIRMATIONS to reprogram your mind and reinforce positive beliefs. Repeat affirmations such as "I am capable," "I am resilient," and "I attract positivity" regularly. Choose affirmations that resonate with you and align with your goals.

Remember, cultivating a positive mindset is an ongoing practice that requires consistent effort and self-reflection. By consciously choosing positive thoughts, actions, and environments, you can foster a positive mindset that supports your well-being and resilience in the face of challenges.

## LEARNING FROM FAILURES AND SETBACKS

FAILURES AND SETBACKS are inevitable in life, but they can provide valuable lessons and opportunities for growth. Here are some ways to learn from failures and setbacks.

### Reflect On the Experience

TAKE TIME TO reflect on the failure or setback. Ask yourself what went wrong, what factors contributed to the outcome, and what you could have done differently. Be honest with yourself and seek insights that can help you avoid similar mistakes in the future.

### Identify Lessons Learned

EXTRACT THE LESSONS and wisdom from the experience. What did you discover about yourself, your approach, or the situation? Identify specific lessons that can help you grow and improve. These lessons can range from specific skills to broader insights about resilience, perseverance, or adaptability.

### Adjust Your Strategies

BASED ON THE lessons learned, adjust your strategies and approaches. Use the newfound knowledge to refine your plans, processes, or decision-making. Consider alternative methods, seek advice from mentors or experts, and be open to trying new approaches. Failure can provide valuable feedback to help you course-correct and move forward.

### Focus on Progress, Not Perfection

SHIFT YOUR FOCUS from perfection to progress. Instead of aiming for flawless outcomes, prioritize continuous improvement. Celebrate the small wins and milestones along the way. Recognize that setbacks are part of the process and that growth is a gradual journey.

### Take Calculated Risks

DON'T LET THE fear of failure hold you back from taking risks and pursuing your goals. Embrace calculated risks that have the potential for learning and growth. Understand that failure is a natural part of the process and that each setback brings you closer to success.

## Persevere and Stay Motivated

USE FAILURES AND setbacks as fuel to persevere and stay motivated. Remember why you embarked on your journey in the first place and let your setbacks serve as reminders of your determination. Stay focused on your goals and keep pushing forward despite obstacles.

## Celebrate Your Resilience

FINALLY, CELEBRATE YOUR resilience and growth. Acknowledge the progress you've made, the lessons you've learned, and the strength you've developed along the way. Recognize that setbacks can shape you into a stronger, more resilient individual.

BY EMBRACING FAILURES and setbacks as opportunities for growth, you can extract valuable lessons, adjust your strategies, and develop resilience. Remember that failure is not the end, but rather a stepping stone on your path to success. Keep learning, adapting, and moving forward with renewed determination.

# EIGHT

# LIVING WITH PURPOSE

*"Life is what we make it, always has been, always will be."*

—GRANDMA MOSES

ONCE, IN A vibrant coastal town, there lived a woman named Grace. She had always been known for her kindness and her unwavering commitment to helping others. Grace had dedicated her life to working at a local animal shelter, where she cared for abandoned and injured animals. Although she found solace in her work, she often felt a sense of restlessness and yearned for something more, something that would provide her life with a deeper sense of fulfillment and direction.

One sunny afternoon, Grace visited a nearby nursing home as part of a community outreach program. She spent time with the elderly residents, listening to their stories and providing companionship. During one of these visits, Grace met an elderly woman named Margaret. Margaret's eyes sparkled with wisdom, and she spoke about her life's purpose with great clarity.

Margaret's story of her younger years as a nurse caring for those in need resonated deeply with Grace. It was as if a missing piece of her life's puzzle had fallen into place. Inspired by Margaret's story, Grace began to reflect on her own life's purpose. She recognized her love for caring not only for animals but also for people.

Over the next few months, Grace embarked on a journey of self-discovery. She attended workshops on healthcare and caregiving and began volunteering at the nursing home. She was amazed at how natural it felt to extend her compassionate care to the elderly residents just as she had done with the animals at the shelter.

As Grace immersed herself in her newfound calling, her life began to take on a new dimension. She felt a profound sense of fulfillment as she witnessed the smiles on the faces of the elderly residents she had come to know. She knew that she was living her purpose, and it brought her a deep sense of direction and contentment.

Grace's life had evolved into a beautiful tapestry of compassion connecting her to the elderly and to the animals she had cared for. Her days were now filled with purpose and meaning as she continued to nurture both her human and furry friends.

As time passed, the ripple effect of Grace's purpose extended throughout the community. Her story inspired others to seek their own sense of purpose, and the town flourished as residents discovered and clarified their individual callings.

Grace's journey was a poignant example of how discovering and clarifying your life's purpose can bring a profound sense of fulfillment and direction. By embracing her purpose, she not only enriched her own life but also touched the lives of many others. Her story served as a reminder that purpose is not just a destination but also a journey, and it is often discovered through the act of serving others with a whole heart.

# MAKING A POSITIVE IMPACT IN THE WORLD

MAKING A POSITIVE impact in the world is a meaningful and fulfilling endeavor. Here are some strategies to help you contribute to positive change.

## Define Your Vision

START BY DEFINING your vision for the kind of impact you want to make in the world. What issues or causes are you passionate about? How do you envision a better world? Clarify your vision and use it as a guiding light for your actions.

## Start with Small Acts of Kindness

MAKING A POSITIVE impact doesn't always require grand gestures. Start with small acts of kindness in your everyday life. Show empathy, compassion, and generosity toward others. These small acts create ripples of positivity that can spread far and wide.

### Volunteer and Support Causes

GET INVOLVED IN causes and organizations that align with your values and interests. Volunteer your time, skills, or resources to support initiatives that make a positive impact. Whether it's environmental conservation, social justice, education, or community development, find ways to contribute to the causes you care about.

### Practice Sustainable Living

ADOPT SUSTAINABLE PRACTICES in your daily life to reduce your ecological footprint. Make choices that promote environmental stewardship, such as conserving energy and water, reducing waste, and supporting eco-friendly products and services. Your individual actions can contribute to a more sustainable future for all.

### Advocate for Change

USE YOUR VOICE to advocate for positive change. Speak up about social issues, injustice, or causes that need attention. Write letters, sign petitions, engage in peaceful protests, or engage in constructive dialogue to raise awareness and influence positive change.

## Support Ethical Businesses

SUPPORT BUSINESSES THAT prioritize social and environmental responsibility. Seek out companies that operate ethically, promote fair labor practices, and prioritize sustainable production methods. By supporting these businesses, you contribute to a more responsible and ethical marketplace.

## Educate and Inspire Others

SHARE KNOWLEDGE, INSIGHTS, and inspiration with others. Educate people about important issues, raise awareness, and inspire them to act. Through conversations, social media, writing, or public speaking, you can have a profound impact on shaping perspectives and motivating others to create positive change.

## Be a Role Model

LEAD BY EXAMPLE and embody the values and behaviors you want to see in the world. Live in alignment with your principles, demonstrate integrity, and show kindness and respect to others. Your actions can inspire and influence those around you to follow suit.

## Collaborate and Build Networks

JOIN FORCES WITH like-minded individuals, organizations, or communities to amplify your impact.

Collaborate on projects, share resources, and pool your strengths and skills. Together, you can create more significant and sustainable change than you could on your own.

### Support Marginalized Communities

BE AN ALLY and advocate for marginalized communities. Educate yourself about their experiences, challenges, and needs. Support organizations and initiatives that work toward equality, justice, and inclusivity. Use your privilege and resources to uplift and amplify underrepresented voices.

### Foster Empathy and Understanding

CULTIVATE EMPATHY AND understanding toward diverse perspectives and experiences. Listen actively, seek to understand different viewpoints, and promote dialogue that fosters respect and empathy. Building bridges of understanding is crucial for creating a harmonious and compassionate world.

### Never Underestimate Your Impact

REMEMBER THAT EVEN the smallest actions can have a significant impact. Every act of kindness, every conscious choice, and every positive contribution matters.

Your individual efforts, combined with the efforts of others, can create a collective wave of change.

MAKING A POSITIVE impact in the world is a lifelong journey. Stay committed, adaptable, and resilient in your pursuit. By living with purpose, kindness, and a commitment to positive change, you contribute to creating a better world for present and future generations.

# CONCLUSION
# LIVING A BIG LIFE

*"The purpose of life, after all, is to live it, to taste each experience to the utmost, to reach out eagerly and without fear for newer and richer experiences."*

—ELEANOR ROOSEVELT

IN THE HEART of a bustling city, there lived a man named David. He had always been content with his life, working at a stable job and enjoying his daily routine. But beneath the surface, a yearning for personal growth had been slowly awakening within him.

One day, David stumbled upon a quote that resonated with him: "The journey of personal growth is the most fulfilling adventure one can embark upon." These words sparked a deep curiosity in his soul, and he decided to explore what this journey might entail.

David started by reading books on personal development, attending seminars, and seeking the guidance of a life coach. He realized that personal growth was not about changing who he was but about becoming the best version of himself. It was a transformative path of self-discovery and continuous learning.

As he delved deeper into this journey, David set goals for himself. He wanted to improve his communication skills, build stronger relationships, and take better care of his physical and mental well-being. Each small step he took was a victory, and he began to see the positive impact on his life.

The path of personal growth wasn't without challenges. David faced moments of self-doubt and had to confront long-held beliefs that no longer served him. But with determination and a growth mindset, he embraced these challenges as opportunities for learning and self-improvement.

David's journey of personal growth led him to new experiences and pushed him outside his comfort zone. He tried new hobbies, met people from diverse backgrounds, and found himself in situations he had never imagined. He realized that personal growth was not just about changing his external circumstances but also about evolving his internal world.

Over time, the transformation in David was evident to those around him. He became a more empathetic and confident individual. His relationships deepened, and his ability to adapt to life's challenges improved. He began to see the beauty in the journey itself, understanding that the pursuit of personal growth was a fulfilling adventure.

The path of personal growth was not a destination but a lifelong journey, and David had come to embrace it with open arms. He understood that the transformative and fulfilling nature of this journey was not about reaching a specific endpoint but about the continuous process of self-improvement and self-discovery.

David's story served as an inspiration to others who, like him, sought personal growth. He had embarked on a transformative and fulfilling path, and in doing so, he had become a living testament to the idea that the journey itself was the true reward.

## EMBRACING THE JOURNEY OF PERSONAL GROWTH

THE JOURNEY OF personal growth is a transformative path that can pave the way for more authentic relationships and experiences in the world around us, as well as help us create lives filled with joy, fulfillment, and purpose. Personal growth requires a commitment to self-awareness, self-reflection, approaching all challenges with a growth mindset, and embracing setbacks as opportunities for learning.

Self-awareness and self-reflection are truly the foundational pieces for personal growth, as they allow you to identify strengths and weaknesses and make conscious decisions for forward motion. When you align the information you've gathered from becoming more self-aware with the goals you've set for improvement, you're left with a custom road map for your personal growth journey along with the motivation you need to succeed. With clear goals in mind, you can meet each bump in the road or failure encountered with a positive attitude and willingness to embrace change and find that these challenges can be approached as lessons to be learned.

Remember that this path of personal growth is rewarding, but not without its trials and challenges. It is important to continuously go back to the foundations of self-awareness and self-reflection as you grow and to remember to practice self-care along the way. As we grow and evolve in our own personal journeys, we build the resilience and mental tools needed to successfully and authentically engage in the world outside our own bodies and minds.

## FINDING MEANING IN EVERYDAY LIFE

WHILE YOU WILL find fulfillment on your journey of personal growth to become your best self, it is important to remember that finding meaning in everyday life can come from extrinsic sources as well. Connecting with the world around us, whether through relationships with others or through independent pursuits, can provide a sense of fulfillment and purpose.

Something you might find while focused on the intrinsic nature of self-improvement is that it is easy to lose sight of the natural gifts that can be found in the here and now of our current situations. That is why it is important from time to time to call on the skills you have learned in practicing mindfulness and gratitude. Take a walk in nature. Savor a cup of tea. Slow down for a moment and take stock of the world around you and the many blessings you have to be grateful for, whether that is the simplicity of a quiet moment or the gift of good health.

Passion and meaning can also be found in action. Pursuing hobbies and experiences that thrill and enliven us is an obvious place to find joy, but don't forget the sense of purpose that can be found in meaningful work and acts of service and kindness to others. Whether this means pursuing a career you love, volunteering in a way that serves others, or simply being open to opportunities to help those around you (like holding a door or letting the family who arrived behind you at the airport pickup take the next available taxi), how you actively participate in your world and community can have a profound impact on not only the lives you touch but your own sense of happiness as well.

One of the most obvious ways to find purpose in our everyday lives is to seek meaningful connections with others. When we actively nurture our personal relationships by connecting in genuine and authentic ways, we begin to build a community of mutual support, accountability, and kinship.

# THE RIPPLE EFFECT OF LIVING AUTHENTICALLY AND INSPIRING OTHERS TO LIVE THEIR OWN BIG LIVES

LIVING AUTHENTICALLY HAS a powerful ripple effect that extends beyond your own life. When you embrace your true self and live in alignment with your values, passions, and purpose, you not only transform your own life but also inspire and impact those around you.

By living authentically, you serve as a source of inspiration for others. Your courage to be true to yourself and follow your own path can inspire those around you to do the same. Your authenticity gives others permission to embrace their own uniqueness and pursue their dreams.

When you practice and promote authenticity in your interactions with others, you are also encouraging others to open up and be authentic in their own lives, fostering a network of genuine and fulfilling relationships. When others experience the realness you bring to conversations and engagements, you create a space for them to be real and vulnerable. Your willingness to show up as your true self encourages others to do the same, fostering an environment of trust and authenticity. This ripple effect enables individuals to feel seen, heard, and accepted for who they truly are. This creates a chain reaction of individuals living more authentically, leading to a collective shift toward a more authentic and fulfilling society.

As you put into practice all of the key lessons you have encountered in this book to promote your own personal growth journey, engage meaningfully in the world around you, and foster healthy and mutually beneficial relationships, you will simultaneously be a beacon of positive influence on others. It may not always be immediately visible or quantifiable, but its impact is profound. By being true to yourself and your personal journey and living authentically, you have the potential to create a ripple effect that spreads positivity, inspiration, and empowerment to those around you and beyond.

Don't be afraid to go beyond leading by example. If you are confident in the positive changes you have created for yourself in your life, don't be shy about sharing your path with others. By offering your guidance, sharing your experiences, and creating a supportive community, you can inspire others to step into their greatness and create a meaningful impact in their own lives and the world around them.

# FINAL THOUGHTS

*"The only person you are destined to become*
*is the person you decide to be!"*

—RALPH WALDO EMERSON

## A SMALL BOOK FOR A BIG LIFE

IT IS MY hope and desire that this little book will enable you to plan and take proactive steps toward living a life of joy and satisfaction. I hope you will set an example to others that success is an action verb and that it is attainable by anyone who has the courage to set a plan in place to attain it. Success is a mindset that starts with gratitude for all the experiences life has to offer.

To say the glass is always half full is a cliché, but it's a cliché based on merit. All those who have followed these steps, either in whole or in part, will undoubtedly benefit from new habits and a mindset that has changed to the positive. In doing so, they will surely enrich every aspect of their lives.

My final hope is simply that when you apply these steps and they become routine and automatic, your life will be enhanced. You will live in harmony with yourself and all those around you, thereby achieving a true state of happiness within you.

The dash on your tombstone is not defined in terms of length, as nothing is promised. It is up to you and you alone to make the quality of the dash. It represents all that you have done, all that you are, and all that you will be remembered for, dear reader. Make it spectacular! Live the dash!

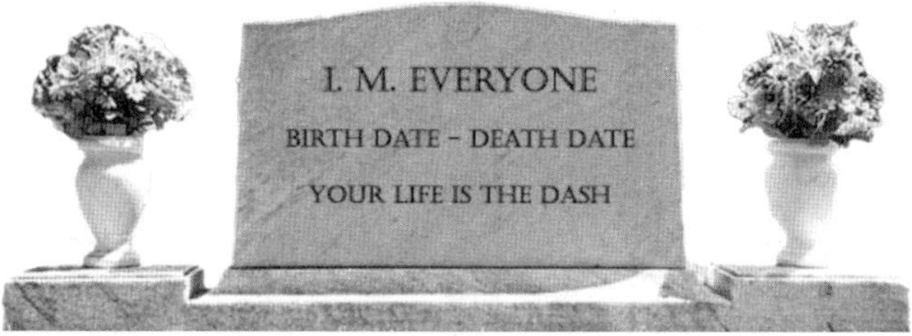


JEREMIAH 29:11